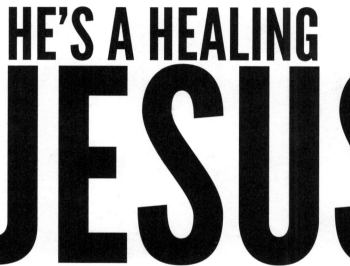

HE'S A HEALING
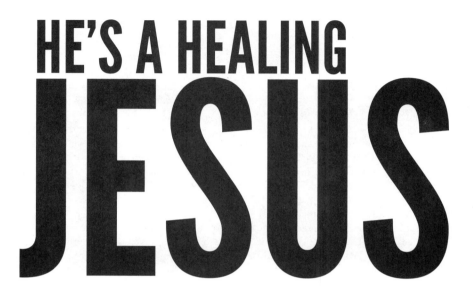
JESUS

by RICHARD ROBERTS

RICHARD
ROBERTS
ORAL ROBERTS MINISTRIES

RICHARD ROBERTS
ORAL ROBERTS MINISTRIES

Published by Oral Roberts Evangelistic Association
P.O. Box 2187
Tulsa, OK 74102

BK2415

ISBN 978-0-9827018-0-5

TABLE OF CONTENTS

WHY I WROTE THIS BOOK

Picture yourself in a room, alone and feeling isolated. You're sick in some way, whether it's physically, emotionally, in your relationships, in your finances, or in some other area of your life. And perhaps you've been that way for quite awhile, like the woman in the Bible who had suffered from a hemorrhage for twelve years. She had spent all of her money on doctors and they'd done what they could do, but Luke 8:43 says that in spite of all that, she *"could not be healed by any"* of them.

Now...picture Jesus knocking on the door of the room you're in and coming inside. He sees you. He knows all about your needs. And He calls your name as He stretches out His strong and loving arms toward you, putting His hand on Your shoulder as you look into His eyes of love and compassion.

As you imagine that scene with Jesus standing next to you, picture Him saying to you, as He said to many when He walked this earth, "What do you want Me to do for you?" With courage and faith in your heart, you answer Him, *"Lord, I want to be healed."*

Now let me ask you a very important question: If the scene above actually happened to you as you've just pictured it in your imagination, *is there any real question in your mind that Jesus would heal you?*

If your answer to that question is, "No, Richard, there's no doubt in my mind that Jesus would heal me if He were right here with me," I want you to know that I've written this book for **you**…to show you how Jesus **is** right there with you, in the midst of what you're going through, every step of the way.

And if the answer to that question is, "Richard, I don't know if Jesus would heal me"…or maybe "Why would Jesus want to heal *me*?" then I've written this book *especially* **for you**. To paint a picture for you of the Jesus I know from His own revelation of Himself in the Holy Bible…the **healing** Jesus…the One who never turned anyone away who came to Him for healing…and who, you can be assured, will not turn you away either.

I'm excited to share with you in this book, perhaps more excited than I've been in a long time. Because I know that many people don't know who the real Jesus is. Their understanding of Him may be based on what other people have incorrectly told them, on some fairy-tale-like image of Jesus that they may have seen portrayed in certain movies, or on the sometimes un–Christlike behavior of those who call themselves Jesus' followers.

But I believe that once you read this book and begin to see for yourself what Jesus is really like—perhaps more clearly than you've *ever* seen before—you'll fall in love with the real Jesus. You'll know that Jesus truly is a *healing* Jesus…you'll begin to see yourself in the light that He sees you…and you'll understand that He *wants* you to be well in every area of your life.

Many times when a book is written, it is dedicated to someone in the author's family or personal life…and I have done that in other books I have written. But *this* book is different. This book I dedicate to **you**, my friend, whom I already see in my spirit as being the way Jesus *wants* you to be, and the way I believe you can be…*healed and whole.*

Chapter 1

WHO IS THE REAL JESUS?

We know from the stories recorded in the New Testament about Jesus' life, when He walked this earth 2,000 years ago, that He was constantly healing people. That's why I can say to you today: no matter what kind of problem you may be facing—whether it's physical sickness, finances, trouble in your family, pain or confusion in your emotions, estrangement or separation in your relationship with God, or something in any other area of your life—**Jesus wants you to be healed and whole**. *He was... is...and always will be a* **Healing Jesus**!

If you're sick in any way right now, know that you are not alone in your struggle. God is on your side. He has promised in His own Word—His revelation of Himself to us—that

- He will never leave you or forsake you (Hebrews 13:5),
- He loves you with a love that will never end (Jeremiah 31:3), and
- Nothing in this world, or any other world, can ever separate you from His love (Romans 8:38).

In fact, God's love for you is so great that He willingly gave His Son Jesus to die on the Cross so that you could come to know Him in a personal relationship right now while you're living, then spend eternity with Him in heaven.

But what God wants for you doesn't stop at salvation, as important and as wonderful as that is. Coming to know Jesus as your personal Lord and Savior is really just the beginning point for what God wants for your life. While you're living on this earth, **God wants you to be healed and whole** in every area of your life!

I can say that to you with *absolute certainty*. I know it's *true*. How do I know it? Because God tells us that in His own words in the Bible…and He tells it to us over and over again.

In Exodus 15:26, God said, **"I am the Lord who heals you."** Notice that God said, "I am the Lord who *heals* you." He didn't say, I am the Lord who *used to heal you* in the past, or I am the Lord who *might heal you* in the future. No. He specifically said of Himself, **"I am** the Lord who **heals** you"—all in the present tense! That means He wants to heal whatever is wrong in your life right now.

You may be thinking, "Well, that might have been true for people who lived in Bible days, but isn't it different today? Things change…people change. Maybe God has changed, too."

While it's true that as human beings you and I are constantly subjected to change in the situations and people around us, the wonderful thing about God is that **He never changes.** He's always the same!

Let's look at what God says about Himself in His Word.

In Malachi 3:6, God clearly said, **"I** *am* **the Lord, I do not change**." Numbers 23:19 NIV says that **"God is not a man, that he should lie, nor a son of man, that he should change his mind**." So not only does God not change in His character, *He never even changes His mind*. And He has never changed His mind about you! He knows what you're going through, and He wants you to be healed.

When you read the accounts of Jesus' ministry in the Gospels of Matthew, Mark, Luke, and John, you can see that He was almost constantly in the process of healing someone, He had just finished healing someone, or He was on His way to heal someone else. Matthew 9:35 tells us that "Jesus went about all the cities and villages, teaching in their synagogues, preaching the gospel of the kingdom, and **healing *every* sickness and *every* disease among the people**."

Matthew doesn't tell us that Jesus healed only people with *certain* qualifications, or that He healed only *certain* diseases or conditions, or that He healed only *some* of the illnesses that people came to Him with. It says that Jesus healed them ALL. Acts 10:38 in the Amplified version of the Bible puts it this way, that Jesus "went about doing good and, in particular, *curing **all** who were harassed and oppressed by [the power of] the devil*."

Jesus never turned away *anyone* who came to Him for healing…and that includes you, my friend. Jesus not only knows what you're going through and has compassion toward you—or as Hebrews 4:15 KJV puts it, He is "touched with the feeling of [your] infirmities"—but *He has the **power** to bring healing to your situation*!

If you've ever wondered if it was God who put sickness, or disease, or some other kind of tragedy on you to begin with, let me assure you that He didn't! In fact, that couldn't be further from the truth. The truth, according to God's own Word, is that it's the devil—the arch-enemy of our souls—who wants to make you sick, and depressed, and isolated from God in your hurting. It's the devil who comes to "steal, kill, and destroy" your life, according to John 10:10. Jesus is the One who came to this earth to bring you LIFE…a life that is "more abundant"— meaning *full* of God's blessings. And He suffered and died on the Cross—taking the punishment that was meant for our sin, and taking on Himself all of our shame, sorrows, sicknesses, and griefs—to make sure you had access to His more abundant life. "He [Jesus] was pierced for our transgressions," Isaiah 53:5 NIV tells us. "He was crushed for our iniquities; the punishment that brought us peace was upon him, and **by his wounds we are healed**."

If you wonder whether sickness is from God or the devil, just ask yourself this question: Is this situation I'm dealing with, something that's **giving** me life....or is it **stealing** from my life? Is it making my life **better**...or is it trying to **destroy** my life? Is it making me strong spiritually, physically, emotionally and in every way...or is it ultimately trying to **kill** me?

Once you answer those questions, it's obvious, isn't it, that sickness is not from God. And, if you have accepted what Jesus did on the Cross for you and you have a personal relationship with Him, that sickness has no "right" to do what it's doing to you—physically, financially, emotionally, in your relationships, or in other areas of your life.

God wants to heal you and make you whole, and He has put His compassion for you inside of me. In just a moment, I want to pray with you and give you perhaps the greatest opportunity you have ever had to really know the One who made you and who has the power to set you free.

But it's important to remember that God will never do anything to violate the free will He has given you. That's why I want to ask you a question that He often asked people who came seeking His healing power. He said, "Will you be made whole?"

You're Part of the Answer

You see, no matter what God wants *for* us, He's only one part of the equation in our healing process. The other part of the equation is *us*. Sometimes we've gotten so used to the situation we're in that we may never have really made the decision that we want out of it.

I remember my dad telling about a man who came to one of his crusades years ago. As Dad talked to him and found out all the things that were wrong in his life, the man said to him, "Brother Roberts, I've been down so long that the thought of getting up has never crossed my mind."

The wonderful thing was that after my dad prayed for him and ministered the love of God to him, the man made the decision that he wanted to have a better life than the one he had been living. And by the end of the crusade, he had not only accepted Christ as his personal Lord and Savior, he had reached out in faith and received healing for his physical body as well.

The first step for his recovery was giving his heart to Jesus and asking Him to save his soul and give him a new start in life. Second Corinthians 5:17 says that "if anyone is in Christ, he is a **new creation**; old things have passed away; behold, all things have become new."

Let's Take the First Step Toward Your Total Healing

Did you know that the greatest healing miracle of all is the salvation of a human soul? Why? Because in one moment's time, God can wipe away the sins and failures of our past and give us a brand-new start in Him. It's as if we are born all over again. We're given a clean, new slate, and a new heart with new desires. We enter into a *personal relationship* with God as our loving heavenly Father, one in which our spirits have been born anew and come alive to Him. Now we have the ability to open our minds and hearts to receiving **all** that He has for our lives.

If you've never taken that first step toward your total recovery… if you've never asked Jesus to come into your heart as your personal Lord and Savior and given Him control of your life, I want to help you do that now. It's not difficult to do; in fact, it's very simple. You can do it where you are right now. It just requires a heart that's sincere before God.

Romans 10:9 NLT says, **If you confess with your mouth that Jesus is Lord and believe in your heart that God raised him from the dead, you will be saved**.

I encourage you to pray this prayer out loud with me right now, and let God open your heart to all He has for you:

> *Lord Jesus, I invite You into my heart today to become my Lord and my Savior. Thank You for dying for me on the Cross at Calvary. I give You my life and ask You to forgive my faults and failures…every sin I've ever committed. I renounce the devil and I turn away from any evil influence I've allowed him to have in my life—whether knowingly or unknowingly. Thank You for loving me and forgiving me. Right now, I receive Your Holy Spirit and Your healing power in my life. Thank You for taking all of my weaknesses on Yourself on the Cross, which includes all my sickness and disease, and for defeating the devil more than two thousand years ago so that I can live in Your abundant life today. Help me to live for You and to be an example of Christ to all those You send across my path. In Jesus' name, amen.*

Salvation…Just the Beginning

I want to tell you about a wonderful testimony that was shared with me many years ago from a man who needed not only salvation, but a multitude of healings in his life. The man's name is Jerry. You may have even heard me mention him on occasion on one of my television programs through the years.

Jerry was a heroin addict and had been in and out of jail for 20 years. One day, he was walking through his apartment on his way outside to find his drug dealer and buy more drugs. He noticed his television set was on. It was tuned to our program… and I happened to be preaching.

As he put on his coat to go out and buy his heroin, I was at the point in my message where I was ready to pray. Through the TV he heard me saying, "Whatever you're doing, stop right now, and let me pray with you."

And though he didn't know why he did it, Jerry stopped in his tracks. He put his coat down for a minute and listened while I prayed. And as I prayed, Jerry began to pray…and that day Jerry accepted Jesus as his personal Lord and Savior. Then the Lord led me to pray for someone who was on drugs. Jerry told me later that when I did that, he felt something happen deep down on the inside of him. And instead of going out to buy drugs as he'd planned, he took his coat off and fixed himself a cup of coffee. Then he lay down on his bed and slept for about eight hours.

When Jerry got up, he felt like a completely different person inside and out. And a couple of weeks later he wrote to me and explained what I just explained to you.

You see, Jerry had been a mainline heroin addict, as well as a drug dealer himself, for many years. His family had literally turned him out because he had become a thief and had stolen everything he could steal to buy drugs. He had stolen his sister's silverware, and even her car, in order to buy drugs. And on top of that, he had been in and out of jail over a twenty-year period for possession and selling of drugs, and for grand larceny. Needless to say, his family felt that in order to protect themselves they could no longer have anything to do with him.

In his letter to me Jerry said, "Richard, I have been off drugs now for two weeks." And he said, "I want you to pray with me that I'll stay off the drugs." So I wrote him back, prayed with him and encouraged him, and gave him some Scriptures from the Bible.

A couple of months later, I received another letter from Jerry. This time he said, "I've been off drugs now for two months. Please continue to pray that I'll be able to stay off." Then six months passed, and the next letter I received was a little different. In this one he said, "Richard, since I've been off drugs, my life has really begun to change."

We continued writing each other back and forth, and within the first year after he accepted Christ and got clean, some major miracles had happened in Jerry's life. First, his family was restored to him. The relationship with his sister, whose car he had stolen, was healed.

Jerry also began giving to God and sending Seed-Faith gifts to our ministry, and God began to multiply his seeds back to him. He was able to get a new car. And the apartment complex where he lived re-established their trust in him enough to ask him to become the manager. So he was able to move into a nicer, larger apartment reserved for the apartment manager.

Jerry got a totally new lease on life…and it began when he gave his heart and his life to Jesus. **I believe that can happen to anyone who allows God to take control of their life.**

Friend, I believe you are standing on the threshold of miracles in your life. When Jesus comes to live in your heart by the power of His Holy Spirit, He brings with Him *all* that He is. And He is so much more than just the One who saves your soul. Remember how He said in Exodus 15:26, "I am the Lord who heals you." Yes, in addition to being our Savior, Jesus is also our **Healer**.

He is our **Provider**, according to Philippians 4:19, for "my God shall supply all your need according to His riches in glory by Christ Jesus." As Deuteronomy 8:17–18 reminds us, we do not give ourselves the ability to make money, it's God who gives it to us, "for it is He Who gives you power to get wealth."

God is also our **Protector**. When we dwell, or consistently *live*, in Him, He becomes our place of protection, or refuge, according to Psalm 91:1–2.

There's a place in the Bible where it talks about God being our Savior, our Healer, *and* our Provider—all in one verse. Psalm 103:3,5 NLT says, **"He forgives all my sins and heals all my diseases. He fills my life with good things."**

God wants to be all those things to you *and more*! But He will never force you to do anything. He has given to everyone "the measure of faith" (Romans 12:3), and He wants us to use that faith to reach out to Him for what we need in our lives. I believe that even now, Jesus is coming toward you, just as He came toward a blind beggar in the Bible named Bartimaeus. And I believe He's saying to you, as He did to Bartimaeus and others recorded in the New Testament record of Jesus' life and ministry, "What do you want me to do for you?"

Tell Him…talk to Him like you would your closest friend. Then watch the miracles begin.

Chapter 2

GOD SEES YOUR SPECIFIC NEEDS... AND HE WANTS TO HEAL YOU

Did you know that God is waiting to hear you tell Him what you want Him to do for you? There was a time in my life when I didn't understand that. And I believe that many people think of God as someone who is too busy and too distant to care about what they're going through. But let's look at the life and ministry of Jesus to see how He dealt with the people around Him, and what He did when He came face to face with human pain and suffering.

In Mark 10:46–52, an account is recorded of Jesus and a blind beggar named Bartimaeus. Jesus was on His way to Jerusalem when He ran into Bartimaeus. Let's read Mark's account of the story and see how Jesus responded to Bartimaeus' need.

> Now they came to Jericho. As He went out of Jericho with His disciples and a great multitude, blind Bartimaeus, the son of Timaeus, sat by the road begging. And when he heard that it was Jesus of Nazareth, he began to cry out and say, "Jesus, Son of David, have mercy on me!"
>
> Then many warned him to be quiet; but he cried out all the more, "Son of David, have mercy on me!"

So Jesus stood still and commanded him to be called. Then they called the blind man, saying to him, "Be of good cheer. Rise, He is calling you."

And throwing aside his garment, he rose and came to Jesus.

*So Jesus answered and said to him, "**What do you want Me to do for you?**"*

*The blind man said to Him, "Rabboni, [or Master] **that I may receive my sight**."*

*Then Jesus said to him, "Go your way; **your faith has made you well**." And immediately he received his sight and followed Jesus on the road.*

With Jesus You're Never Alone

I want you to see this man for a moment because he represents many people today who feel like life has passed them by. Throughout my ministry of praying for people for more than 30 years, I have become aware that people who are critically ill, or who have been sick for a long time, *especially* feel that way. I hear from many of our Partners that not only are they dealing with physical illness, but the isolation and loneliness they experience on top of it just makes matters worse.

That must have been how Bartimaeus was feeling that day. Not only was he blind, but because of his blindness he had been forced to become a beggar to eke out a meager living for himself. He must have felt alone in his struggle. He must have known that he was on the fringes of society, isolated and not accepted by those around him.

That's what Satan does to human beings. He tries to steal from you—from your health, from your relationships, from your finances and other areas. He tries to *isolate* you from other people, to tell you that you're not as good as they are…that you're not even worthy of God's love and concern. Often he uses other people to help him do that. As Bartimaeus heard that Jesus was coming near to where he was, he must have had a glimmer of hope, because the Bible says he cried out to Jesus, "Son of David, have mercy on me."

Wouldn't you think that when those around Bartimaeus heard him yelling for Jesus, they might have helped him? That they might have even picked him up and carried him to Jesus, making sure Jesus saw him and had the opportunity to minister to him? But that's not what happened, is it? Not only did they not help Bartimaeus, they actually tried to silence him by warning him to keep quiet.

It's as if they were saying to Bartimaeus, "Don't bother Jesus. He's too busy to be concerned with the likes of you." It's as if they were actually trying to kill any hope he had of getting out of the situation he was in and someday having a better life.

Maybe you're feeling like that right now. Perhaps someone, even in your own family, has discouraged you from thinking that you could ever be healed and whole again. Or maybe you've somehow gotten the mistaken idea that God doesn't even know you exist…and if He does, He doesn't really care about you anyway.

My friend, I want to declare to you right now that based on what God shows us in His Word, that simply couldn't be further from the truth. He not only knows about your situation, but He's ready and willing right now to help you get out of it. Let's look at how Jesus dealt with Bartimaeus…and the people around him who were trying to keep Bartimaeus down.

Jesus Responds to Our Cries of Faith

When Jesus heard Bartimaeus crying out to Him, the Bible says that Jesus "stopped," or as The Message version puts it, "Jesus stopped in His tracks." That's right. The God of the universe put on hold what He was doing when He heard someone in need calling out to Him. He could have just kept walking. In fact, He could have walked right past Bartimaeus, patted him on the head, and gone on down the road. But that's not what Jesus did...and it's not what He will do when He hears you crying out to Him in faith, either!

To the very people who had tried to shut Bartimaeus up, He commanded them to tell him to come to Him. At that point, they suddenly changed their tune with Bartimaeus. Now they even encouraged him to cheer up! They said, "Hurry. Get up! Jesus is calling you." And they were ready to help him come to Jesus.

And it's very interesting what Bartimaeus did next. The Bible says that he "threw aside his outer garment, jumped up, and came to Jesus."

Even before anything else happened, Bartimaeus took off his beggar's robe and threw it on the ground. And that's a very important thing to remember. Because in those days, people who were beggars—who had permission from the local government to beg for a living—wore a certain kind of outer garment. I don't know if it had stripes. I don't know if it had checks. I don't know what color it was, but it was a certain type of garment that showed that they were legally a beggar. When they had the garment on, it identified them as being at one of life's lowest stations.

When we have a problem, or a serious sickness—maybe one even called "incurable"—or some other kind of failure in our lives, how easy it would be to just "park" there. How easy it would have been for Bartimaeus to do that...to park beside his blindness, and his station in life as a beggar.

But the message of the Gospel shows us that he didn't do that. It says that when Bartimaeus heard that he was going to stand before Jesus of Nazareth, he threw off his beggar's robe before even meeting Jesus. It was as if he threw down his old life *in preparation and expectation for receiving something new from Jesus.* He must have heard about Jesus, and the miracles He was performing!

As soon as Bartimaeus came before Jesus, Jesus said something to him that was very important…and something that shows what the true nature of the Lord really is. Jesus could have said, "I'm very busy. What do you want?" in a surly way, as people sometimes do.

But Jesus looked at Bartimaeus with kindness and compassion, and He asked him, "What do you want Me to do for you?" Jesus was used to people coming to Him. He could have just said some kind of quick "blessing" over Bartimaeus and been on His way. But Jesus **saw** Bartimaeus…He saw him as an individual, and He was interested in Bartimaeus' individual needs. And that's how Jesus feels about you. He cares about your individual desires and needs.

It appears that Bartimaeus was certainly ready to tell Jesus what he needed from Him. Can't you just see him throwing down his beggar's robe with the full force of his faith, standing before Jesus, and answering Him clearly, as He declared, "Master, I want to see!"

And Scripture shows that there wasn't even *a moment's hesitation with Jesus.* He immediately said to Bartimaeus, "'Go your way; your faith has made you well.' And immediately he [Bartimaeus] received his sight and followed Jesus on the road."

Now, wouldn't it have been sad if Jesus had said to Bartimaeus something like, "Well, Bartimaeus, you'll have to come back some other time. I already healed one person this week and I'm fresh out of healing power right now." Or what if He'd said, "Maybe God made you blind in the first place, and maybe He wants you to stay that way."

Sounds like the way some people think about Jesus, doesn't it? I know people who think that way and you probably do too. That's why we can't make people our Source. God may use them as instruments in our lives, but we must never make them our Source. *Only God can be our Source.* People will let you down. That's just part of our human nature. We need to remember that, and always make God alone our Source.

If you've listened to people who aren't sure about Jesus' healing power, or they aren't sure if Jesus really wants to heal you, I want you to remember what Jesus said as Bartimaeus stood before Him. He said, "What do you want Me to do for you?"

What Will Your Answer Be?

I believe Jesus is asking you that same question right now: "Carol…or John…or Mary…or Jim…what do you want Me to do for you?"

Is it cancer that you need Him to heal? Is it arterial sclerosis? Is it arthritis? Is it a problem with your knees…or pain in your back…or a heart problem…or some other physical problem?

Is it a problem in your family that needs restoring? Is one of your children on drugs? Is someone being abused? Are you going through a separation or a divorce?

Maybe you've lost your job and you need employment. Or you're wondering where your next house or rent payment is coming from.

Or do you need to get back on track in your relationship with the Lord? Maybe you've backslidden and need to go back to church. Or maybe you've hurt someone, or someone has hurt you, and there needs to be repentance and forgiveness, and you need healing for the hurt.

Whatever it is, Jesus is asking you, "What do you want Me to do for you?" He's asking you, just as He asked Bartimaeus in the Bible, because **He's still a healing Jesus. He hasn't changed**. And He wants to heal *you* and make you whole.

Acts 10:34 tells us that God is no respecter of persons, which means He doesn't "play favorites." His healing power is not just available to certain people at certain times...but *it's available to everyone.* If He ever healed anyone—and we know He did because many healings are recorded in the Bible—He's still healing people today.

I know people who question whether or not it's God's will for us to be well. And when they pray for someone who's sick, or they are sick themselves, rather than just asking God to heal them, they say words to this effect: "Lord, *if* it be Your will, please heal this person." I think possibly the reason why some people pray that way may be because they've interpreted a couple of Scriptures in the wrong way.

The first Scripture that may be misunderstood is in Matthew 8:2–3, where we're told about a leper who came before Jesus. Leprosy was a slow death sentence in those days, and people who had it were generally ostracized and separated from the rest of the population. You can imagine that if you had it, you'd be desperate for healing if you heard of someone, like Jesus, who had the reputation of having the power to heal the sick.

This particular leper came to Jesus and said, "Lord, You can heal me, *if it be your will*"—in other words, **if you *want* to**. Notice that Jesus didn't hesitate. He didn't have to think about His answer. He didn't have to stop and wonder, "Do I want to heal him, or don't I?" He *immediately* said to the leper, "I **will**...or "It's my will to heal you." Today, He would say it like this, "Yes. I **want to** heal you."

The second Scripture that is often misinterpreted, or wrongly applied, is in Luke, chapter 22, when Jesus was in the Garden of Gethsemane, knowing that He was about to face torture and death, and He prayed to His Father, "Lord, if it be your will, let this cup of death pass" (v. 42).

In that instance, Jesus wasn't talking about anything to do with healing. He was talking about how, in His human flesh, He didn't want to go to the Cross to cut a new covenant in His shed blood, because He knew He was going to have to suffer and die to do it. Though He didn't want to, He was still willing to obey His Father. He knew it was God's will. He knew that's why He came. He knew He came to die that you and I might have life and have it more abundantly. He knew He was going to have His back bloodied and striped that we might be healed from the crown of our heads to the soles of our feet.

He wasn't talking about whether or not it was God's will to *heal*. He was talking about His own humanness. He didn't want to do it. Finally He said, "Nevertheless, at your will, I'll do it." And aren't we glad He did? Aren't we glad He went to the Cross? It's exactly *because* of Jesus' suffering and death on the Cross that you and I can be healed today. First Peter 2:24 says, *By whose stripes you were healed.*

Scripture leaves no question that it is God's will to heal us, in every area of our lives. In fact, He calls it His highest wish. "Beloved, I wish above all things that you may prosper and be in health, even as your soul prospers," is what 3 John 2 tells us.

It's very important for you to know that it's God's will to heal you—that He wants you to be well—or you may never exercise your faith to receive His healing power in your life when you need it most.

If you're sick, or if you need to be set free from any kind of dis-ease in your life, and have wondered if God really *wants* to heal *you*, I believe He's stirring your faith right now. As you've read these words, you may have felt something different in your spirit than you've felt before. Maybe you didn't have the hope before to believe for healing…and now you do. The Bible tells us in Hebrews 11:1 that hope is the very thing that our faith is built on, for *faith is the substance of things hoped for, the evidence of things not seen.*

I encourage you right now to reach out to the Lord for the healing you need. I want to pray a prayer of agreement with you, and become your partner in faith to believe God for the miracle you need.

Let's Pray:

Father, thank You for telling us clearly in Your Word that You want to heal us...that You sent Your Son Jesus to die on the Cross in order to bring us healing in every area of our lives. I join my faith now with the one reading these words, and together, we claim Your healing power for whatever sickness, or family problem, or emotional stress, or other situation has been trying to destroy his or her life.

Friend, right now, I speak directly to that thing that the devil has been bringing against your life...and I command it to be gone, and never to return, in Jesus' mighty name. Lord, we give You all the glory, and thank You for the miracle You're performing. In Jesus' name, we pray. Amen.

I encourage you to begin checking yourself to see if there's something you can do now that you couldn't do before. If you couldn't bend your leg, try bending it now. If you couldn't lift your arm up above your head, try lifting it now. If you're believing for a financial healing, begin looking in the mail or answering your telephone and expecting to find God's miracle provision for you. Every day, continue exercising your faith and expecting God to continue the process of your total healing.

If the miracle you need didn't happen instantly, that doesn't mean God's answer isn't on the way. Once when Lindsay was sick and needed healing, she had my dad pray for her to be healed. When their prayer was over, Lindsay seemed just the same as she was before. But my dad told her not to be discouraged. He told her of the story in Luke 17 where two lepers that Jesus had prayed for were healed "as they went" (v. 14). Meaning, they were healed as they left Jesus and went on with their lives. Dad told Lindsay not to be concerned about not being healed instantly, and he encouraged her that she was "went-ing"—or being healed *as she went* about her life. And sure enough, that's exactly what happened. Before long, as she went about her life, Lindsay was healed and feeling as good as new.

Instant miracles are wonderful. That's what we all want...and I've seen many of them through the years in my ministry. I've experienced a few myself. But most of the time, it seems that healing comes to us more gradually. And it may be that way because God knows we need healing in another area of our lives, as well, for us to really recover and hold onto the *total* healing He wants us to have.

Whole Person Healing

Have you ever noticed how a microwave oven heats food so hot that sometimes you can't even touch it without burning your hands? When we expect a "microwave"—or instantaneous— miracle, maybe God knows that sometimes it would also be too "hot" for us to handle. We may need time to allow Him to work in other areas of our life so that we can hold on to our healing, and not lose it as soon as our faith is challenged in some way.

God doesn't want us just to feel good emotionally one moment, and lose our healing in the next. He wants to heal us in our whole person. I believe that's part of what He's telling us in 3 John 2 when He says that He desires us to be healed, *even as our **soul**—our mind, will, and emotions—prospers.*

In Jesus' ministry, a blind man was brought to him once in a town called Bethsaida. In Mark 8:22–25 we're told that after

Jesus touched the man and prayed for his eyes, *He asked him if he saw anything. And* [the man] *looked up and said, "I see men like trees, walking."* In other words, his eyesight was improved, but he wasn't seeing everything clearly. *Then* [Jesus] *put His hands on his eyes again and **made him look up**. And he was restored and saw everyone clearly.*

I think it's very possible that the blind man needed more than just his physical sight healed. He needed his spiritual sight healed, as well...or perhaps the way he looked at life. Notice that the second time Jesus touched his eyes, it says that He made the man "look up." Maybe the man was used to looking down in his life. Maybe he had a down outlook about life and even the people around him. But when Jesus touched his eyes a second time, notice it says that he was restored and "saw everyone clearly."

Lindsay explains it like this: She says "sometimes we need time to press into God and allow Him the time it takes for our complete healing, inside and out."

No matter how our healing comes to us, God knows best what we need. And often when it requires us to use our faith over time to become an active participant in our own healing, it may be the best healing we ever receive.

I encourage you to stay in a state of expectancy for your miracle. I believe that miracles are coming toward us or going past us all the time. Later in this book, I want to talk to you more about how important it is for us to "pull down" or put a claim on what we want from God. But for now, just remember that when we stay in a state of expectancy, we are much more able to be aware when God is working a miracle in our lives, to receive it when it comes, and thank Him for what He has done...and we're much less apt to let it pass us by.

Chapter 3

GOD PUT HIS COMPASSION FOR YOU IN ME

There's another important reason that I know in my heart that God wants to heal you...and that is because *He put His compassion for you inside of me.*

For more than 30 years, I have prayed for the needs of hurting people. I have traveled the world and seen that people are the same everywhere—from the busy streets of New York City, to the tiny huts of a "cardboard city" in Central America, to the slums in African nations. God has shown me that everyone is hurting in some way. It may not always be a physical need that we're facing, but all of us have areas in our lives—or in the lives of our loved ones—where something is causing pain.

In Matthew 14:14 we're told, "And when Jesus went out He saw a great multitude; and He was *moved with compassion* for them, and *healed their sick.*"

Jesus had gone to a place where He could have some time alone to rest and spend time praying and communicating with His Father. But the crowds of people found out where Jesus went and they followed Him there. They knew He was performing miracles and so they followed Him everywhere: the deaf, the blind, the dying, even those who couldn't walk or talk were often brought by others to where Jesus was—like the man in Mark 2:1–5 who was paralyzed and couldn't walk on his own. Four of his friends made a stretcher for him and carried him to where Jesus was. When they got there, the crowds were so great, they couldn't even get inside to where Jesus was. Desperate to get their friend help, they tore through the roof where Jesus was and lowered their friend down to Him.

What does the Bible record about that incident? Does it say that Jesus was upset with them for interrupting His ministry? Does it say that the man and his friends went home no better off than when they had come?

If ever Jesus had the right to say to someone, "Be gone. I'm too busy to deal with your problem right now," it was that day, in that situation. But that's not how Jesus responded. Scripture shows that Jesus did two things:

- He saw the faith of the man's four friends, and
- He healed the man.

Did you know that God can see your faith? You may be in a situation right now where nobody can see your faith. They may be able to see your illness or the way the illness has affected you. But when you reach out to Jesus, Jesus not only sees the situation you're in, but He *sees your faith*. And He is moved with compassion toward you.

Isn't it wonderful to know that we serve a God of compassion, and not a God of anger or wrath? When Jesus came to this earth and lived as a man, He experienced everything we experience as human beings. Speaking of Jesus, Hebrews 4:15 tells us that He "understands our weaknesses, for he faced all of the same testings we do."

Yes, He is moved with compassion towards us. But compassion doesn't mean what some people think it means. While compassion does have an element of sympathy in it, it is so much more than *just* sympathy alone…for sympathy alone really never helped anyone get out of the situation they're in. No, compassion makes you *want to rid the person of their sickness or other situation they're facing.* And that's what Jesus did when He went to the Cross.

Jesus didn't come to this world just to say to us, "Oh, you poor things. I feel so sorry for you being lost and apart from God, and being a target for the devil to harass and intimidate." No! His compassion for us moved Him to die on the Cross in our place so that we might be saved…healed…and delivered once and for all. His compassion moved Him to action…and it still moves Him to action today.

For years when I was growing up, I would watch my dad be moved with compassion for the sick. I remember being by his side many times in the great tent cathedral when he would reach out his hands and pray for the sick for literally hours at a time. In the invalid tent—a smaller tent outside of the main tent where people brought those who were too sick to go through the prayer line—I saw Dad pray for all kinds of people with all kinds of conditions. Many of them had been given up on by the medical profession because there was nothing else that could be done for them. Often they came for prayer as a last resort. Everything they had was riding on being prayed for by Oral Roberts.

I'll never forget being with Dad once when he came near a man with terminal cancer. The man had been brought to the invalid tent in a hospital bed. The cancer was so advanced, you could smell the terrible, putrid smell of death all around him. The smell was so strong, in fact, that Dad had to turn his face away and vomit. He didn't know if he could even stay near the man long enough to pray for him. He said, "I can't do this. It's too hard."

But as Dad began to walk away, God spoke to him as strong as he ever heard Him speak, and He said, "If you are not willing to pray for this man, you are not worthy to be My child." I never knew until much later that God had said that to him. I only saw my dad whirl around toward the man, take him in his arms, and pray for his healing.

Dad put everything he had into ministering to the sick. By the time a service was over, He was often so tired that he would have to be helped back to his hotel room where he would collapse in exhaustion. Yet I've heard him say that he would rather pray for the sick than eat food when he was hungry.

That's what the compassion of Jesus is like for *you* when you're hurting. I saw it in my dad, and I know from my own personal experience of praying for the sick all these years. When you let the compassion of God flow through you and allow yourself to be led by the Holy Spirit, He pulls you toward a person's need...until you want to do everything you can to help them be healed.

When I was in the Central American nation of Nicaragua, I was loaned a car and a driver to take me around where I needed to go. One day in the car the driver, who spoke only Spanish, began to talk. I didn't know what he was saying, but my interpreter told me the driver was saying, "My mother needs prayer."

Well, whenever I hear words like that, I tune everything else out...because, to me, prayer time can happen anytime and anywhere. And it does! People often come up to me for prayer—it doesn't matter whether I'm at the grocery store, at a friend's house, or in a restaurant. If someone is hurting, I'm ready to pray. And by the way, people come up to me for prayer all the time, no matter where I am.

That day in the car, when I heard the driver say that his mother needed prayer, I could almost imagine how Jesus felt when He heard Bartimaeus cry out of the crowd, "Lord, have mercy on me!"

I asked my driver, through the interpreter, "What's wrong with your mother?" In Spanish, he began to tell me, "My mother has had back pain for many years."

"Where does she live?" I asked. "Can I go and pray for her?"
"No," he answered. "She lives six hours from here."

As he said that, I remembered the Scripture in Psalm 107:20 that says, "He sent his word, and healed them, and delivered them from their destructions."

I knew that God was in our car. I also knew that God was in his mother's home. So I said, through the interpreter, "If you can get your mom on the phone, I will pray for her right here in the car."

He was so thrilled. He was driving with one hand through the incredible traffic of the city of Managua, and dialing the phone with the other...which I wouldn't generally recommend. But I've learned that sometimes God does very unusual things!

The driver got hold of his mom and put her on the speaker-phone so we could hear each other. He told her who I was and that I wanted to pray for her. Though she couldn't speak a word of English, she began to talk and talk. It reminded me of the Bible story in Luke 8 of the woman who had suffered with "an issue of blood"—a problem with hemorrhaging. She had been sick for 12 years and had spent all of her money going to doctors for help, though they hadn't been able to help her in the end. I imagine if she had told Jesus all the truth of her situation, she might have gone on talking for an hour! Just like her, my driver's mother had a lot to tell.

Through my interpreter, Edgar, I was able to know when she finally got to the point where she was talking specifically about her back. Through him I asked her, "How long has it bothered you?" She said, "I've had pain for 10 years," and I saw her son nodding his head. Then I said to her, "Señora, I'm going to send God's Word to you."

Well, what good would that do? you might be saying to yourself right now. *You're in a car...you're driving in major traffic, and you're just going to reach your hand out and speak the Word. You don't even know where this woman is!*

But isn't that what Jesus did when the Roman centurion came to Him in Matthew 8:5–13? He told Jesus that one of his military aides was very sick. When Jesus said, "I'll come and heal him," the centurion answered Him by saying, "You don't need to come, Jesus. You just send the Word." As a military officer, he understood the concept of authority, and he knew that when he gave an order it was obeyed. He believed that if Jesus "spoke the Word," or gave the order, his aide would be healed. And we're told in verse 10 of that passage that Jesus marveled, or was amazed, at what great faith the centurion had. He'd never before seen faith like that, even among the Jews.

Jesus *did* send the Word. And you probably remember what happened. The aide was healed! We're told in verse 13 that he was healed, just as the centurion had believed, that very hour. The Amplified version of the Bible even says that he was healed "that very moment," when the centurion believed.

So there is Bible precedent, or example, set by Jesus Himself, to send the Word to someone when you can't be there to pray for them in person.

Through my interpreter, I said to this woman, "I'm going to send the Word to you," and I began to pray. For some reason, God had me focus on the instrument panel of the car. And when I did that, something happened. That car became like the sanctuary of a church...a holy place. The speedometer, odometer, and other parts of the instrument panel just seemed to disappear...and in its place, I saw the woman's back.

Now, how can that happen? you ask. I don't know. I just know that right in the middle of where the instrument panel had been one minute before, I now saw her back instead!

The woman was six hours away. But remembering that there's no distance in prayer, I reached out toward where I saw her back, and I said, "In Jesus' name, I speak to this back pain, come out!" And over the phone I could hear her shouting! Then I said to her, "You're beginning to feel something warm now," because the Holy Spirit told me that. He let me know so I could tell this woman.

She said back to me, "Yes, I feel warmth."

I said, "Start bending."

She answered, enthusiastically, "I am. I am!"

We praised God together, and I had the driver take me back to my hotel. About three hours later when he picked me up for the evening crusade service, he had a smile all across his face... from one ear to the other. He told me, "After 10 years of back pain, my mother is now completely healed!"

Because of the love and compassion of God that flowed through Jesus, He never turned anyone away who came to Him for help or healing. The Bible tells us in several places that "**He healed them all**." (See Matthew 4:24, 12:15, and Luke 6:19.)

He has put that kind of compassion inside of me for you, and for all those who come to our ministry for prayer. Jesus would be walking somewhere and somebody would run up and grab Him, wanting to be healed. Or He'd be on His way to pray for somebody and someone else would stop Him and say, "My daughter's dying. You've got to come!" and He had to be ready, always ready, to minister to them.

I feel that same strong urging always to be ready to pray for people. I can't walk by someone sick without praying for them, even if they don't know I'm praying. I can't walk by somebody in a wheelchair without trying to get up close to them so I can pray for them. I have found that the compassion of Jesus always pulls me toward a person's needs. When Jesus is involved in your ministry, you're not repelled or put off by people's needs. You want to help them, in the same way Jesus would...and that is to bring them healing.

It's *Your* Time to be Healed

Right now, I feel drawn in my heart toward *your* needs. And I know that the compassion I have is coming from the compassion of Jesus flowing through me…for you.

I send the Word to you, as I did to the woman whose back was healed. I command whatever affliction Satan is bringing against you to be gone.

Now, stir up your own faith to reach out to Jesus for healing. Imagine Jesus walking toward you, as He did toward Bartimaeus, and saying to you, "John…Mary…What do you want Me to do for you?" Because that's what He's doing through me. Then tell Jesus exactly what you want Him to do. Be specific with God. Don't just say, "I need healing." *I believe when we get specific with God, He gets specific with us.*

If you need *physical* healing in your body, tell Him **where** you need healing, such as: "Lord, heal my left eye. It's blurry and I can't see out of it very well." If you need *emotional* healing, tell Him **why** you need healing, such as: "Lord, my marriage is falling apart and my heart is broken. Please heal my relationship with my husband…or with my wife…and help me become a better spouse."

Tell God everything in your life that needs His healing touch. Don't hold anything back. **God has more than enough healing power to meet every one of your needs**. Don't ever feel like you can only ask Him for certain things, or that you have to ask for just one thing at a time. The way we act sometimes, you'd think that if we ask God for too much we're going to bankrupt heaven. That couldn't be further from the truth!

God's resources are unlimited, and He wants to meet every need in your life; I believe He's just waiting for you to ask Him. James 4:2 says, *You do not have because you do not ask.*

Right now, I encourage you to ask God for whatever healing you need. Some people may believe that the words you say when you pray are the most important thing. But I believe it's the attitude of the heart that counts—that we speak to God honestly out of our hearts just as you would talk to a friend—and that as soon as we ask for healing, we release our faith to Him and begin to expect the answer…whether it comes right now, later today, tomorrow, next week, next month, or whenever. And any time you receive a physical healing, I strongly recommend that you go back to your doctor and let him or her confirm the healing. When you're truly healed, the healing will stand up to any tests your doctor can give you, and the confirmation of your doctor just makes your testimony stronger.

I would love to hear about any healing you experience, particularly as you're reading this book, so I can rejoice with you. You can let me know about it by several different methods. You can:

1. **Log on** to our website at: **www.oralroberts.com**. At the top of our homepage, click on *Praise*.
2. **Call** the Abundant Life Prayer Group at: 918–495–7777, any time—24 hours a day/7 days a week.
3. **Write** me at: Richard Roberts, P.O. Box 2187, Tulsa, OK 74102–2187.

Not only will sharing your testimony encourage me and other people (if you give me permission to share it), but it is a very powerful way to encourage your own faith and to remind yourself what wonderful things God has done for you. Your personal testimony also gives you the "spiritual ammunition" you need for any future spiritual battle you may face. Revelation 12:11 tells us, "They overcame him [the devil] by the blood of the Lamb and by the word of their testimony." So don't ever forget that your personal testimony is a very powerful weapon you have at your disposal.

In fact, I believe that our testimonies of healing—or simply telling someone else what God has done in our lives—are what often can give people the hope they need to be healed themselves. Testimonies help confirm what God has said in His Word and remind us that God is still doing in these days what He did in Bible days, and that is healing those who come to Him in faith. I pray that as you share your testimony of what God has already done, or is doing, in your life, your faith will be encouraged and your spirit will be strengthened to believe God for the healing you need.

Chapter 4

GOD TAILORS HIS HEALING POWER TO FIT YOU

Now that we've established that God wants to heal you, based on God's own Word about Himself, let's look at some of the different avenues that He may use to heal you.

In my experience through many years of praying for the sick, I have seen God heal people in many different ways, through many different methods. He is not limited to just one way of healing. He deals with people as individuals. He is not a "cookie-cutter" kind of God. In fact, **I believe God tailors His healing power to fit the needs of the person who is hurting**.

One of the questions I'm often asked about healing is: "Is healing only by the Holy Spirit, or does our faith have a role to play in it?" Well, we know from Scripture that God is the Source of all healing, and there is only one Healer…God Himself. Man has no healing power in himself. I certainly don't. I'm just an instrument that God uses. I cannot heal anyone myself. If I could, I would empty out every doctor's office and hospital in the world. But I don't have the ability; only God does. So we know that all healing comes from God.

But we can also see from the Bible that our faith has a role to play in healing.

- To the Roman centurion in Matthew 8, Jesus said, "Go your way; and *as you have believed*, so shall it be done."
- To the woman with the issue of blood in Luke 8, Jesus said, "Your *faith* has made you well."
- To the two blind men in Matthew 9, Jesus said, *"According to your faith*, let it be done unto you."
- And to the Syrophonecian woman in Matthew 15, Jesus said, "Great is your *faith*. Let it be done even as you have prayed."

So Jesus was saying that our faith definitely has a role to play in healing.

And to help activate your faith, I believe it's helpful to know some of the different ways, or methods, that God often uses to bring healing to us...because I believe He tailors His healing power to fit each person.

Medical Care

One of the most obvious means that God uses to help us receive healing when we're physically, or sometimes emotionally sick, is the wonderful care that doctors and other medical professionals can provide. Jesus Himself said, *They that are sick need a physician* (Luke 5:31, paraphrased).

I remember hearing my dad talk about having tuberculosis as a teenager and how many good, Bible-believing people didn't believe in going to doctors back then. And even though I think the numbers of Christians who feel that way today are much smaller, I know there are still many who may believe that God heals *only* through supernatural means.

But I don't believe that God makes a distinction between the natural and the supernatural in the way that you and I often do. You see, when God created the world, He put all the ingredients in the earth that are used to make medications—men may have developed those ingredients, but it's important to remember that it was God who put them there in the first place. And when you read the first chapter of Genesis, you can see that God said that *everything* He had created was "good." That means that everything God created had a good and holy purpose behind it.

Then through the ages He has called gifted and caring men and women into the medical profession who are dedicated to making people well. Many of them love the Lord with all of their hearts and know that when they treat their patients, it's God alone who has the power to heal. As they practice, they know—just as I know when I pray—that they are just instruments in God's hands.

Why would God have given us everything we need to make medications that often save people lives, and called doctors, nurses, and others into the medical profession to take care of His people, if He didn't intend for us to take full advantage of those things?

So God knew there would be times when we would need the help of doctors and their good medical care. Did you know that one of the Gospel writers, Luke, was a doctor? That right. For a time, Dr. Luke and the Apostle Paul traveled together preaching the Gospel and caring for the hurting. As a doctor, Luke had a unique perspective about the healing ministry of Jesus that you can see running through the Gospel of Luke and the book of Acts recorded in the New Testament.

For years, our ministry has tried to follow the Biblical model of *combining* God's healing streams of both medicine and prayer. When I travel around the world to a foreign nation to preach the Gospel, I always take a medical team with me—a team of doctors and nurses and others, sometimes as many as 20 people—to minister to the physical needs of the people. I love the quote attributed to Gandhi—who obviously was not a born-again Christian, but a believer in the Hindu religion—when he said that "even God would not appear to a hungry man except in the form of bread."

I believe he was echoing the words of Jesus in Matthew 25:35–40 when He said, *'I was hungry and you gave Me food; I was thirsty and you gave Me drink; I was a stranger and you took Me in; I was naked and you clothed Me; I was sick and you visited Me; I was in prison and you came to Me…Inasmuch as you did it to one of the least of these My brethren, you did it to Me.'*

I believe that people cannot always hear the Gospel message being preached when they are starving for food to eat, or thirsty for clean water to drink, or sick from lack of sanitation and in need of medications to help them get well.

Many of the people that we see in our free medical clinics do not have access to medical care until we arrive, and with the distribution of simple parasite medications, or shoes to wear on their feet, or antibiotics, vitamins, and minerals, they can begin to live healthier lives. Others are malnourished or starving, and with nutritious meals given to their families, they can continue to work and earn a small living for their loved ones.

Those acts of kindness and compassion show forth a good God to people who may never have known Him before. They show Someone who cares about *all* of their needs, not just spiritual needs alone, so that when the Gospel message is preached in my healing services, they can finally hear the truth. Then with hearts that have felt the love of God in a concrete, undeniable way in their lives, they can finally reach out in faith to receive that life-transforming message.

We have been so blessed to have access to good-quality medical care in this country. So many people around the world either have no access or cannot begin to afford to go to a doctor, even when one is available.

I believe in using all of the means that God has provided for us to be healthy—whether we consider them to be natural or supernatural. Good nutrition, adequate amounts of sleep, exercise, controlling our levels of stress, regular medical and dental checkups, Christian counseling, the prayer of faith, the laying on of hands—and other methods I will talk about in this chapter… all are wonderful means God has given us for our good health and well-being. And when we learn to combine them together, as God intended us to do, I believe we have a better chance of living a healthier and more productive life for Him.

Laying On of Hands

One of God's methods of healing I was most familiar with as I grew up was the **laying on of hands**—one of the methods spoken of and demonstrated in the Bible.

The reason why I was personally acquainted with it was because that's the method God gave my father to use. Oral Roberts laid hands on the sick; he would physically touch those that he prayed for. And the Bible tells us in Mark 16:18 tells us that we believers *shall lay hands on the sick and they shall recover.*

There are some people who think we should not lay hands on people anymore. But didn't God tell us to do that in His Word? Those who don't believe in doing it say, "Well, that was a word for Jesus' disciples." And I agree with that. But the problem is in stopping just with them…because Jesus told us in John 8:31 that if you and I continue in His Word, then *we* are also His disciples today. We're not one of the original 12 disciples, but we're one of the millions who follow Jesus today. So we have a right and an obligation to do what God told us—His modern-day disciples—to do, and that is to lay hands on the sick and to believe they will recover.

When you read about Jesus' public ministry in the Gospels, you see that He often touched the people He was ministering to.

• He touched the blind man in John 9 when He rubbed his eyes with the mud He had made by spitting on the ground… and the man's blind eyes were opened.

- He touched Jairus' daughter in Mark 5 when He was told that she was dead, and He told her to sit up…and the little girl sat up and was healed.
- He touched Peter's mother-in-law in Matthew 8 when she was lying in bed with a high fever…and the fever left her. She was so well, in fact, that it says she got up and prepared a meal for Jesus.

The Bible doesn't indicate that Jesus touched everyone who came to Him for healing, and sometimes when He touched someone He combined His touch with a command of faith that He would speak directly to the disease or condition affecting the sick person. But laying His hands on people was one method He often used to bring healing…and it's one method He still uses today. And He does it through people like you and me.

Now laying my hands on people is not the primary way the Holy Spirit operates through me. He most often works through me by using my mouth and my voice as I *speak the Word* to people from the platform or wherever I am ministering. But God often works through my hands, as I lay them on people and pray. And recently—especially since I turned 60 years old and the anointing of the Lord has come on me in a new and fresh way—I have felt the power of God moving through my left hand, and God has led me to touch people more than ever before.

When I talk about the importance of laying hands on people to pray for them, someone will often say to me, "You have a special call to the healing ministry." And I do have a call to the healing ministry of Jesus Christ. But as a person, I'm no more special than you. And certainly my hands are not special. They're just instruments that God uses, as He will use anyone's hands, when we yield them to Him in humility and obedience. My hands don't heal. But when I lay them on someone and release my faith, praying in Jesus' name, then my hands become an extension of the hands of Jesus. But it's not me. It's never me; it's Him. And I give Him all the glory.

I remember once, years ago, when I was in the African nation of Ghana. The President had invited me to come to his office for a news conference. And he and I stood there before the media of the nation and they broadcast it live on Ghanian television.

When the news conference was over, I said, "Mr. President, can I pray for you?" He said, "Yes." So we joined hands together and prayed. But when the prayer was over—I said amen and he said amen—he wouldn't let go of my hand. And it was unusual. With him being a bigger man than I was and having a hand half again as big as mine, I couldn't get my hand loose. He just stood there holding my hand, while we were on live national television.

It was awkward for a moment. Then he said to me, "Reverend Roberts, I've touched many hands in my life, some hands hot, some hands cold. But your hand has the right temperature."

Then I understood what had been happening. He had felt the presence and power of God through my touch…and he didn't want to let that go. I said, "Mr. President, I think I know what you're trying to say, but it's not me. It's the anointing and the power of the Holy Spirit that you're feeling, and I am just the instrument."

There's just something special about the touch of a human hand, when it's combined with the love and compassion of Jesus, and done respectfully and in humility before God. I believe it can open us up to the healing power of God and help us believe for a miracle.

If you need healing today, I encourage you to find a church, or a prayer group, or a circle of friends, or even one person who will pray for you regularly and will lay their hands on you in faith, believing that when they do you will recover. When you combine your faith together and use this very powerful and Bible-honored way of praying for the sick, I believe God will honor your faith in reaching out to Him for a miracle.

Praying for Someone Else's Healing

The second method that God often uses in our healing is found in James 5:16 that says, *Pray for one another, that you may be healed.* **When you pray for someone else's healing, that healing can come back to you**. Why? Because you're being obedient to God's Word...and because when you pray for someone else you're planting a seed *for yourself* that can bring you a powerful harvest from God.

Many people read the Scripture in James 5:16 this way, *Pray for one another that* **they** *may be healed.* That's not what this says. It says, *Pray for one another that* **you** *may be healed.* That means that when you pray, don't *just* believe that God will heal the person you're praying for, believe that He will heal **you** too.

I'll never forget when a woman who worked for our ministry was diagnosed with cancer. Her doctor told her there was nothing that could be done medically, and that she had about six months to live. That woman wanted to be healed, and she felt God leading her to pray for as many other people who had cancer as she possibly could. She believed that her own healing would somehow be connected with praying for others.

So she began to follow God's leading. She prayed for as many people as she knew personally who had cancer. Then she often went to hospitals and prayed for those with cancer. She often went to minister to people even when she wasn't feeling well herself. Her healing didn't happen overnight. But it wasn't long before the woman began to get better physically. The reports from her doctor improved, and each day she felt stronger and stronger...until one day she was pronounced completely cancer-free!

There is power in praying for one another! There's power in **agreeing together in prayer**. In Matthew 18:19–20 Jesus tells us, *If two of you shall agree on earth as touching anything that they shall ask, it shall be done for them of my Father which is in heaven. For where two or three are gathered together in my name, there am I in the midst of them.*

I believe there are times when we need someone else to help us…when we need the faith of another believer to help bolster, or hold up, our own faith when we're fighting a spiritual battle and believing God to bring victory over sickness or some other situation in our lives.

There was a popular song years ago called "No Man Is An Island." One line of the song said, "No man is an island; no man stands alone. Each man's joy is joy to me; each man's grief is my own."

I believe Jesus taught us this concept over and over in the Scriptures, when He said things like:

- Pray for one another (James 5:16),
- Forgive each other (Colossians 3:13), and
- Bear one another's burdens (Galatians 6:2).

I believe praying for one another is a powerful method of healing that was tailor-made for the Church. Can you imagine what would happen in churches around the world if this were done every Sunday, in every congregation…where the pastor would have people turn to the people around them for two minutes and pray for one another's healing? Just imagine the miracles that would happen!

I personally know there are some churches who do take a few minutes in each service to pray for one another…or they have a special time of prayer for each other at the end of their service.

If you don't already attend a church like that, I want to encourage you today to find one. Find a church that believes in the Word of God, that believes in the power of prayer and agreeing one with another. Let others help lift you up and fight the good fight of faith with you. Deuteronomy 32:30 teaches us that "one can chase a thousand, while two can put ten thousands to flight" (paraphrased).

At first glance, you might think that Scripture says that if one can chase one thousand, then two can chase *two thousand*. That would make sense if you're just "doing the math," as the expression goes. But God tells us that when two people join together, they are *more than doubly* as powerful…they're at least **ten times more powerful** than one person battling something alone. And that's just the power in two people joining their faith together! What if you joined your faith with a large group of people…or a whole church full of people? That's why it's important to ask other people to pray with you.

And that's why we have our Abundant Life Prayer Group available for prayer 7 days a week, 24 hours a day. There's never been a time since it was founded more than 50 years ago when prayer for those who call us has not been going up from the ALPG, night and day.

I want to encourage you to call the Abundant Life Prayer Group at **918–495-7777 any time** you need someone to join with you in prayer. Sometimes in the middle of the night, there isn't always someone you can get hold of for emergency prayer. Especially at times like that, the Abundant Life Prayer Group can function as your 24-hour spiritual emergency room. When you call them, they will agree with you in faith right at that very moment. They will help you stay strong in faith and encouraged through the Word of God to continue believing God for miracles. Then they'll forward your prayer request on to me and Lindsay and we will pray for you as well. Together, we will come into agreement with you for the answers you need, and we will stay in agreement with you until your miracle comes.

Speaking the Word

When the Roman centurion came to Jesus for his servant's healing in Matthew 8, Jesus offered to come and heal his servant. But the centurion—somehow, as a soldier with an authority of his own—understood that Jesus' authority extended far beyond just His physical presence, into even the words that He spoke. And he said to Jesus, "If You just **speak the word**, my servant will be healed" (verse 8).

Now some people prefer to call this method of healing **"sending" the Word**, based on Psalm 107:20, *He sent his word, and healed them, and delivered them from their destructions.* And if you heard me preach, you've probably heard me refer to it both ways, because it's talking about the same thing.

I'm personally very familiar with this method of healing because I'm asked to do it all the time, especially as I'm often praying for people over television and I can't be with them in person. So I stretch my hand out toward the TV screen, and I send the Word—or proclaim the promises of God's Word out loud—to people for their healing. And I often tell people watching at home to stretch out their hand toward my hand, or lay their hand over my hand on their TV or computer screen, as a point of contact to release their faith for a miracle.

Someone might say, "That's crazy!" No. I'm not basing it on what I think. I base it on what the Bible says in Acts 19:11 AMP, that *God did unusual and extraordinary miracles by the hands of Paul.* Paul was a follower, a disciple, of Jesus. But Paul's not here anymore, and what Paul could do I can do, as Jesus' disciple today. And since I can't be with most of the people I pray for, according to the Bible I have the same authority Paul had to stretch out my hand toward you and have you stretch out your hand toward me so that we can have a "faith touch," as I'm speaking the Word for your healing.

Really, I use it as a means to help people get their faith moving and get it into action. I hear from many who tell me that it was just the point of contact they needed to help them release their faith for a miracle.

But even without extending my hands, I believe my voice carries the authority of the Word of God into any situation. When I first began my healing ministry in 1980, God began working through me in a way that was very different from my dad. Dad always touched people when he prayed, as I've mentioned before. But I felt God instructing me to use my voice instead and simply speak out His Word of healing to the people.

Often God gives me supernatural knowledge about someone He is healing in the audience, whether it's over TV or in person. Sometimes it comes through an impression or just a knowing in my spirit; sometimes I might "see" something in my spirit, as I did the day I was praying for my driver's mother in Nicaragua and God showed me her back in the place of where the car's instrument panel was. Or sometimes I feel something in my body, physically.

When I first began to pray for the sick, I didn't always understand what God was doing, especially when I would feel something strange in my body. It happened with the first person who was ever healed in one of my services.

I was in Albuquerque, New Mexico, and Lindsay and I had been believing God for a healing ministry to begin to manifest in my life. I had felt the calling to pray for the sick when I was just a boy. But through the years, as I rebelled against living for God or having anything to do with the ministry that my father was involved in, I had let go of that dream and replaced it with another: that of becoming a professional singer and athlete. I was very good at both, and was on my way to fulfilling that dream.

Then, God got hold of my life when I was 19 years old and I gave my heart to Him and really accepted Jesus as my Lord and Savior for the first time as an adult, as I dedicated my life to Him. I began working with my dad in the ministry, and gradually God re-kindled that original dream He had put inside of me to pray for the sick. But I never had the faith or courage to step out into a healing ministry until after Lindsay and I got married and we began to join our faith together and "call" that dream into reality by "calling those things that be not as though they were" (see Romans 4:17).

So Lindsay and I had been going about our daily lives from the time we were married, thanking God for the healing ministry we believed He was bringing into my life. Then in April 1980, it happened.

I had been traveling and preaching for some time. And I would often say a general prayer for healing at the end of my services. But nothing specific ever happened that I was aware of. Then in a service one night, we had a wonderful time in the Lord. It was almost over and I was getting ready to leave when all of a sudden I felt a cracking and popping in my big toe! Well, I knew there was nothing wrong with my toe...and all of a sudden I heard myself saying out loud, "God is healing someone's big toe."

For a few seconds, I was in shock! I couldn't believe I'd just said those words out loud, for everyone to hear. And I realized that if no one responded, I would look like pretty bad...like a failure, or maybe even like I was just making the whole thing up. But I knew I wasn't. I was sure God was healing someone's big toe...even when no one stood up or came forward in the service.

We left and went home, not knowing what had really happened. And for several nights, when I would go to sleep all I could see in my mind was someone's big toe! I just kept seeing it and seeing it...and it kind of bothered me. But I went on with my life. What else could I do?

Finally, one day the mystery was solved. I received a letter from a man who said, "Richard, I'm the person with the big toe you were talking about that night! The doctor's X-ray showed that I had broken my toe and it had been hurting. But that night during your service, I felt my toe pop...and it hasn't hurt since. Then my doctor confirmed with another X-ray that my big toe was completely healed."

I knew it! I knew God had been giving me a sign in my body that someone's toe was being healed. And sure enough, it was. That was the way my healing ministry began 30 years ago. And that is still the way God sometimes deals with me in letting me know that He's healing someone. I will get a sign in my physical body, or a knowing will come into my spirit, and I know I am to speak that word out so that someone in the audience can receive it by their faith and be healed.

I've come to understand that those things are an operation of the word of knowledge—one of the nine gifts of the Holy Spirit listed in 1 Corinthians 12:4–11, that I'll talk more about in the next section of this book—and I have to speak them out in order for people to receive what God is doing, and be healed.

I believe that sometimes people think a word of knowledge is similar to magic—that somehow speaking that word out loud means that someone is just "magically" healed. But I believe that once that word is spoken out, it must be "claimed"—in faith—by someone who is believing God for a miracle. Think of that spoken word in the same way you would think of being notified that you had inherited a certain amount of money or real estate from a rich relative. While it's true that the inheritance is yours and it belongs to you, unless you step forward and "claim" the money, or the real estate, or whatever it is, you might never actually be in possession of it.

Just as it's essential for you to claim your inheritance in the natural to actually take possession of it, it's essential to claim your spiritual inheritance—or those things Jesus died on the Cross to give us: salvation, healing, deliverance, etc. That's the part that God expects *us* to do. We can have all the faith in the world inside of our hearts. But James 2:20 tells us that *faith without works* [corresponding actions] *is dead.* If we put no *action* to the faith we have in our hearts, many of the blessings God offers to us will never be ours. Jesus did all He could do by dying on the Cross for your healing and mine. Now, there's something for us to do… and that is to use our faith to claim our healing.

Stretch Out Your Faith and Receive God's Word to *You* Now

If you're hurting right now, I'm going to speak the Word for your healing. As I do this, I am stretching my faith out toward you…and I want you to stretch your faith out toward me. You might even want to stretch your hand out toward this book, or lay your hand on yourself as a point of contact to help your re-lease your faith for a miracle. Remember what I said earlier, that this is not magic; it's the Word of God…and when you activate your faith and let it go toward the One who is your Healer, it means that you're agreeing with that Word. And as we go into agreement with God's Word and with each other, by our faith, I believe powerful miracles will happen.

Let's join our faith together and agree with God's Word, as I speak forth the word for your healing. Be sensitive to the Holy Spirit's moving in your life, as I pray. And reach out and claim *by your faith* that spoken word for whatever area you're hurting in.

> *In the name of Jesus, I send the Word to you right now. I speak to back pain and I command it to come out. I speak to pain in your legs. I send the Word to your legs and I command the pain you've been experiencing to come out.*
>
> *I speak to the problem with your heart. I send the Word to your heart to beat normally, and for any clogged arter-*

ies to open up. To every heart problem I say, come out, in Jesus' name.

I speak to problems in your eyes. Cataracts, be dissolved. Macular degeneration…glaucoma…blindness or loss of vision of any kind, come out. I send the Word to you who are suffering a loss of hearing and command your ears to open.

Breathing problems…problems in the joints…addictions to drugs, alcohol, pornography, abuse, or any other kind…I command you to come out now. Blood pressure, blood sugar, in Jesus' name be healed. Every cancer, tumor, cyst, and growth, come out now, in the name of the Lord.

*I speak to pain in **any** area of your body, whether it's in your knees, your back, your shoulders, your legs, your stomach, your chest area, your head…wherever it is, and I command that pain to be healed…and never to return again, in Jesus' name.*

Release your faith right now for a miracle!

Now begin to check yourself. That's right. Go ahead and check yourself. Can you tell a difference? Is there something you can do now that you couldn't do before? Can you bend or move in a way you couldn't do earlier? Perhaps you're hearing better, or seeing better than you were just a few minutes ago. If so, begin to give the Lord praise for what He's doing, and continue checking yourself later on and trying to do things you couldn't do before.

Healing can come, as I've said before, *instantly*. It can come in such a strong way that there is an instant change in your body or your circumstance where it is very clear to you, and even to other people, that you have been healed. In fact, it would almost be impossible to deny it. I know of cases where someone was healed who wasn't even actively seeking it at the time. God sometimes uses healing as a sign to an unbeliever that He is indeed God, and a miracle like that may turn a person's heart toward God that was not inclined that way before experiencing a miracle.

But that is not always the way healing happens. In fact, it seems to be more the exception than the rule. It seems that in order to be healed, or to receive any blessing that God is trying to send our way, it's important for us to get our faith moving and into action of some kind in order for us to receive it. And as the devil would like to keep you sick and keep you from ever being healed, there is a constant, invisible battle raging against you.

Any time you are believing God to heal you and someone prays for you or speaks the word to you for healing—physical healing, in particular—I encourage you to activate your faith by trying to do something you couldn't do before. I believe God wants us to be an active partner with Him in our healing.

As I just prayed, even if I didn't mention your particular problem or situation, I believe you can still "put a claim" on your healing. Sometimes when I receive a word of knowledge and speak that word out, seemingly it is for one specific person, or one specific condition…but other people will respond with their faith and receive their healing, as well. For instance, when I'm in a church or auditorium, I may feel as if the word of healing I am speaking is for someone in a particular section of the building…and people in another section will be healed, also. Or I may speak a word that someone is being healed of cataracts…and there may be someone, or even several people, who are healed in their backs or some other area of their bodies, in addition to the cataract healing.

Why? I believe it's because they "piggy-backed" their faith. The healing I was speaking out *was* for the specific person I felt it was for, and they came forward and testified to that fact. But other people attached *their* faith to it, as well. In their spirits, they said, "That healing is mine!" and, sure enough, they were healed.

Another thing that often happens when I speak the word for healing is that *later on*—maybe days later or even weeks—I will hear from people who tell me that they are now healed, and they believe their healing started when I sent the word, or spoke out the word, to them.

Remember the story in Mark 11:12–25 where Jesus spoke to a fig tree outside the town of Bethany and commanded it to wither and die. The disciples heard Him say it, and they went on with Jesus to Jerusalem. When they passed by the fig tree again on their return trip the next day, they paid special attention to it, and excitedly told Jesus that the tree He had cursed had withered and died. When they did, Jesus reminded them that when they prayed, anything was possible to them if they truly believed in their hearts and did not doubt it would happen.

When Jesus first spoke that word, it seemed as if nothing happened on the outside of that tree. But the reality is that something was happening on the inside. When they passed by the tree the next day, it had dried up from the roots.

Remember that when someone sends the word to you—maybe even over television, as I do on my program as the Lord leads—or if you're in a service where someone speaks a word of healing and you believe it's for you and claim it for yourself, don't get discouraged if nothing appears to be happening on the *outside* immediately. Don't discount what may be happening on the *inside* that may take a little time to be manifested on the outside. Just when you're thinking, "Maybe God hasn't touched me yet," remember the fig tree that Jesus spoke to. *He may be touching you right now, and you just can't see it in the natural yet. That's the time to keep the eyes of your faith open.*

There's an old expression we use sometimes, when someone is doubting what is true in the natural and they just haven't seen it yet. That expression is: *seeing is believing.* With faith, the opposite is often true: **believing** *is seeing*. So don't give up on God…and don't give up on His healing power coming your way.

Anointing Oil

James 5:14–15 tells us another Bible-honored method of healing. It says, *Is anyone among you sick? Let him call for the elders of the church, and let them pray over him, anointing him with oil in the name of the Lord. And the prayer of faith will save the sick, and the Lord will raise him up.*

This was a common practice in the early Church. When someone was sick, the "elders," or leaders, of the church would be called on to anoint them with oil and pray for God to raise them up. The oil was seen as a symbol of the Holy Spirit's power, and the act of anointing was done to consecrate or to "set apart" the sick person to God. In other words, they were acknowledging that God was the Source of all healing and that He alone could heal. I believe the act of anointing with oil reminds us of the healing power of God that is available to us, through His Holy Spirit, when we reach out to Him in faith believing.

In those early days, there were no church buildings where people would gather to worship, as there are in many parts of the world today. Believers would usually gather in their homes to worship God together. So the leaders of the church were often close by and could easily come to pray for someone who was sick and anoint them with oil for healing.

Today, it may not always be that easy to have the leaders of a church available to pray for those who are hurting. Or there may be people who are unable to attend church because they're either home-bound, caring for someone who is, or they're dealing with some other issue that is preventing them from going to church. That's one of the reasons for our Abundant Life Prayer Group, where you can call for prayer any time of the day or night. James 5:16 also encourages *all* of us, whether we're leaders or not, to *pray for one another.* And we can keep a little vial of anointing oil in our homes to use to anoint ourselves or someone else when they're sick or in need of some kind of healing prayer.

Many years ago we began offering small vials of anointing oil through this ministry. My dad and I would pray over the oil that came to us in large barrels, then we would take that prayed-over oil and have it put in small vials that could be sent out in the mail to those who requested it. Now there was no power in the oil itself. It was just a kind of common cooking oil that you might have in your own house. But when my dad and I prayed over it, we believed that it became the container, or the delivery system, that carried the power of our prayers to those who would use it to anoint someone who was sick. Or they might even use it to anoint themselves.

As we offered it on our TV program and in our publications, the response was tremendous. Hundreds of thousands of people wrote or called in and requested our anointing oil. Over time, we began to hear back from many of them about how, after they used the anointing oil and had someone pray for them, they were healed.

Here are two wonderful testimonies we received some time ago from people who had used our anointing oil to pray for their loved ones in need of healing. The first one is from a woman in Texas who told us this story about her sister-in-law who could have lost a foot to amputation. This is what her letter to us said:

> *Thank you for sending me your anointing oil. My sister-in-law is a diabetic and had carelessly gone eight years without any medication at all. She was eating and drinking sweets to her heart's content. Then she stepped on a nail that went into the big toe of her left foot. She didn't see a doctor right*

away, which she should have done, but went on for about three weeks without telling anyone what had happened.

By the end of those three weeks, my sister-in-law was so sick she couldn't get out of bed in the morning. She was burning up with fever and her left foot and leg hurt all the way up to her hip. My brother quickly took her to the doctor, who immediately made preparation to hospitalize her for surgery. He said he would have to amputate at least half of her left foot, if not all of it.

I don't have to tell you how she and her family took that news; it wasn't good. The night before she was to enter the hospital, I anointed her with the oil you sent me, and I did it again early the next morning before she left home. I told her I'd be praying for her speedy recovery and reminded her to have faith in God's healing power.

Praise God, she didn't even require surgery at all, and was able to go home right away. She was absolutely thrilled and so thankful to God for her healing. Isn't it amazing what a little faith will do...mixed with prayer, and a little vial of precious anointing oil?

The second testimony is from a woman in Oklahoma who needed the miracle of a new heart. Here's her exciting story:

I had a chronic heart condition that my doctor had been treating for several years. One Sunday evening, I thought I was dying. I had an awful feeling...I became so weak that my legs just crumbled underneath me, and nothing seemed to be functioning normally.

I called our doctor, but he was out of town and wouldn't be back for another week. But I needed help right then! I thought of my little vial of anointing oil your ministry had sent me. And I said, "Lord, please help me," as I dipped my little finger in the oil and rubbed a small amount of oil over my heart.

When I did that, a wonderful feeling came over me. My legs became strong again, and I felt like my whole body had been cleansed all over. I rested good all through the night and felt fine the next morning.

When my doctor got back in town, I went for a check-up. After tests, he said, "I can tell you that you've had a cardiac arrest—a heart attack. But everything looks normal now. Can you tell me what happened?" I told him my experience with the anointing oil and prayer, and he was as amazed as I was at the miracle I'd received.

I haven't had any more trouble with my heart since. Using anointing oil was a new concept to me, but I know now that the Bible teaches us to do that. I've used it several times now. Many times it seems I have used almost all my precious anointing oil, but the last little bit never seems to run out! Thank you for helping me understand how God can use something as simple as a little bit of anointing oil to bring healing into our lives.

Today, we still offer anointing oil that Lindsay and I have prayed over to our friends and partners who request it.* As our own children were growing up, every night we would anoint them with oil and pray over them. Occasionally, if we would get home late or were very busy with a hectic schedule, they would come get us before going to bed and remind us to anoint them with oil and pray. This family practice became very important to them...and to Lindsay and me. We believe it's one of the things that helped our girls stay safe and healthy and just generally blessed by the Lord all while they were growing up.

You might want to consider setting aside a few minutes like that every day for yourself, if you're alone, or for you and your spouse or other family members. Just anoint yourself, or your loved one, with a little oil—and you can use any cooking-type oil you have in your home, if you don't have anything else.

What you can do, and what is customary for many people to do, is to put a tiny bit of oil on your fingertip. Then use that finger to trace a small cross on yourself or your loved one's forehead, or near the place where they may be hurting or in pain, and say something like: *I anoint you in the name of the Father and of the Son and of the Holy Spirit, and I ask God to heal you, in Jesus' name.* You can be more specific in your prayer if you know what the specific need is, but if not you can say a simple general prayer, like the one I mentioned.

When the Bible tells us specifically to do something—as it tells us to anoint those who are sick with oil and to pray for them—I believe there is power in obeying God's Word. We may not always understand why things happen in the supernatural or how they work. But time and again, I have seen that anointing with oil is one of the Bible-honored methods that God often uses for healing those who are sick.

To request a free vial of anointing oil from the Oral Roberts Ministries, call **918–495-7777**, *or go online to* **www.oralroberts.com/bookstore**.

Prayer Cloth

Another method I have often seen God use in healing people is through the use of a *prayer cloth*. In Acts 19:11–12, we're told, *God gave Paul the power to perform unusual miracles. When handkerchiefs or aprons that had merely touched his skin were placed on sick people, they were healed of their diseases, and evil spirits were expelled.*

Many people wanted Jesus' followers to come and pray for them, because their prayers had powerful effects on the sick. In

Acts 5:15, we're told that new believers would sometimes bring those who were sick and lay them in the streets when Peter was going to be passing nearby so that his shadow could fall on them and they could be healed. And many people were healed that way.

Tradition teaches that the Apostle Paul was in a certain area, and there was an epidemic in another area, so Paul could not go and lay hands on them. Acts 19:11–12 indicates that cloths that he had been carrying were taken to people to lay on those who were sick, in the place of Paul who could not be there. God used that method to heal many sick people. The power of God was so strong, in fact, that even people who were filled with demon spirits were delivered when one of the "prayer cloths" was laid on them by someone who was releasing their faith for a miracle.

So the use of prayer cloths is not something weird or something that someone just made up. It is a Scripture-based, Bible-honored way of praying for the sick.

For many years we have made prayer cloths available to the partners of our ministry, or to anyone who contacts us and requests one.* We pray over the cloths and anoint them with our prayers to carry God's healing power to people. We give them away free and encourage people to use this Bible-honored method of healing if they or someone they love is sick or in need of any kind of miracle from the Lord.

As I always remind people when I'm talking about the use of prayer cloths—or anything else that we use to help release our faith to God—God can use any method to heal those who reach out to Him in faith. But we must never get our eyes on the method; that is, we don't put our faith in the cloth, or the oil, or any other point of contact. We must keep our eyes on Him who *alone* is the *Source* of all healing.

One of the best and easiest ways to understand a prayer cloth is that it's like a "container" or a "delivery system" for healing prayer. There's nothing magical about the cloth itself; it's just plain ordinary material like you could find anywhere. But when we pray over it in faith, that plain ordinary cloth becomes a delivery system for carrying God's healing power to you, when you combine *your* faith with ours.

The wonderful thing about a prayer cloth, or a little vial of anointing oil, is that you can use it as a point of contact to help you set the time and place you're going to release your faith for a miracle. I believe a point of contact can be important in receiving your miracle.

Think of it this way: you and a friend run into each other on the street one day. You haven't seen each other in a long time and would really like to catch up on your relationship. So before you part company, you say, "Let's get together for lunch sometime." But then when you get home neither one of you ever calls the other one to decide on a time and place to meet for lunch. If that's the case, you'll probably never actually get together for lunch, will you?

But if one of you tells the other, "I'll call you next Monday and we'll pick a lunch date" and you do that, the chances of actually going out to lunch with your friend greatly increases.

Well, that's similar to how a point of contact works. It can help you be more specific in releasing your faith and believing that when you use the point of contact—whatever it may be— you can be healed.

Now a point of contact can be many different things. But for many of our partners, anointing oil and prayer cloths seem to be tremendously helpful. We constantly receive testimonies from people who tell us how they, or one of their family members, received tremendous miracles when they used the anointing oil or a prayer cloth I sent them to help release their faith.

In fact, I want to share a story with you right now about a couple who are partners of this ministry, and also friends of Lindsay's and mine, whose child became very seriously ill years ago when she was small. Using a prayer cloth we had sent them from this ministry made all the difference in their child's miraculous recovery.

Here's the testimony, as told from her father's viewpoint:

God Had a Plan for Our Child and Now She's Living It!

When our firstborn child, Whitney, was about nine months old she was diagnosed with a rare blood disorder that made her very sick. Over the months doctors tested her blood, but the test results were never satisfactory. Her condition just seemed to be getting worse.

One evening we heard a stirring in her bedroom. I went in to pick her up, and when I felt her head she was burning up with fever. We took her temperature and watched the thermometer go from 102 to 106 in a short period of time. We knew it was a very serious situation.

Just moments later she started to go into what looked like some kind of seizure. My wife ran to the kitchen to dial 911 and get an ambulance to come right away. As I was holding Whitney in my arms, she went limp, as we sat there for what seemed like an eternity.

The paramedics examined her and explained that she had had a febrile seizure, or a seizure caused by a high fever. Thankfully, she was stabilized for the moment, but we were told to get her to a doctor as soon as we could the next morning.

At the doctor's office the next day, they ran a battery of blood tests. And they found out that her red blood count was way below where it should have been. Whitney was very pale, and her mom and I were very frightened and concerned. Finally we were told that if it didn't improve quickly, they would need to do a blood transfusion on our baby. Back then, with all the concern there was about blood purity, our little daughter having a blood transfusion was a pretty scary thought.

Just a day or two earlier, we had received a prayer cloth in the mail from the Oral Roberts Ministries. And the thought came to me about the woman in the Bible who'd had an issue of blood for 12 years, and was healed when she reached out and touched the hem of Jesus garment. (See Luke 8:43–48.)

So we let Whitney sleep with that prayer cloth the rest of that night. We prayed over her and we said, "Lord, we need a miracle, and we need it now." We united ourselves together and agreed in faith that we were going to have a healing. We knew God's Word was true. We knew Jesus had already died on the cross for all sicknesses and diseases, and we believed He was going to heal her. We just knew our daughter's healing was done when we put that prayer cloth on her. And it was!

When we went back to the doctor on Monday morning, her blood was perfect! We've had it tested many times since then, and it's been perfect ever since.

Years later, when Whitney was 13 years old, she traveled to Mexico on her first missions outreach team, ministering to children in needy areas. Our daughter is a young woman now. We knew that God had a plan and purpose for her life. And we're so grateful that she's able to live it.

As Whitney's parents knew, it wasn't the cloth that healed their daughter. There was no power in the cloth itself. But it was symbolic of the healing touch of Jesus. It wasn't Jesus' robe that healed the woman in the Bible with an issue of blood. It was Jesus. And when we use prayer cloths to help release our faith for healing, we always need to remember that it's not the cloth that's important. It's not the fact that I hold them in *my* hands and pray over them before giving them to people. As you release your faith and look to God for healing, a prayer cloth can become an extension of the *healing hands of Jesus.*

I want to encourage you to consider using a prayer cloth, or whatever you believe God may be leading you to do to help release your faith to Him. God heals people in so many different ways and by so many different methods. He knows us so intimately and so individually that He knows the best way to help us any time we reach out to Him in faith.

*To request a FREE Prayer Cloth, call 918-495-7777, or log on to www.oralroberts.com/bookstore.

Chapter 5

WHEN WE ACCEPT JESUS' SACRIFICE ON THE CROSS, HEALING BECOMES OUR RIGHT

In this chapter, I want to talk to you about something that I believe is very important to your healing. Unfortunately, it's something that is also commonly misunderstood by Christians: **I want to talk to you about the significance of Jesus' death on the Cross.**

I believe that until the full meaning and implications of this all-important event are understood, many believers will continue to live on earth plagued with all kinds of afflictions, sicknesses, sorrows, and fears. It's because of our ignorance of what Jesus really did on the Cross that many of us fall short of the expectations we should rightfully have for ourselves as Christians, and for all of God's people. Because only those who understand the essence of Jesus' death and resurrection can appropriate, or claim for themselves, its full benefits.

Jesus lived a life of righteousness, or a life comprised of only doing good for others...and He did it without ever committing sin, or living in any kind of disobedience or rebellion toward God, His Father. While He lived on earth—until He was 33 years old—He healed the sick, freed the captives, and brought peace and victory to the brokenhearted. But the scope of His earthly ministry—because He allowed Himself to be fully human—was limited by time and space.

But Jesus achieved much more in His death than He did in His life, and that's really saying something! The Bible indicates that He continually went about doing good, healing all who were oppressed by the devil (Acts 10:38). Jesus died on the Cross of Calvary for two reasons: 1) to pay the ransom, or price, for our sin, and 2) to live inside of us through His Holy Spirit.

Jesus is omnipresent—meaning that now He's present everywhere at the same time, always available to save those who accept Him as their Lord and Savior and to minister His healing and delivering power to those who reach out to Him in faith.

Ransom for Sin

The most dramatic expression of God's love to the world is the redemptive sacrifice of His only Son, Jesus, on Calvary. His suffering on the Cross opened the way of blessing to mankind...the way God had originally intended us to live before Adam and Eve rebelled against Him in the Garden of Eden and introduced sin into the human race. As Paul wrote in Ephesians 1:7, we are accepted by Christ *in whom we have redemption through His blood, the forgiveness of sins, according to the riches of His grace.* Therefore Christ's death on the Cross at Calvary represents the ransom, or price, that God paid for the sins of man. In other words, Jesus *bought us back* through His suffering and death, and He *brought us back* into the relationship of blessing with His Father that was intended for us from the beginning.

By Jesus' sacrifice on the Cross, He bore all our sins, transgression, suffering, sickness, and shame, in fulfillment of the prophecy in Isaiah 53:4–5 AMP. *Surely He has borne our griefs (sicknesses, weaknesses, and distresses) and carried our sorrows and pains [of punishment], yet we [ignorantly] considered Him stricken, smitten, and afflicted by God [as if with leprosy]. But He was wounded for our transgressions, He was bruised for our guilt and iniquities; the chastisement [needful to obtain] peace and well-being for us was upon Him, and with the stripes [that wounded] Him we are healed and made whole.*

Think of Jesus' sacrifice in terms of how He took the place of Barabbas, a man condemned to death. Barabbas was a notorious criminal, armed robber, rebel, and murderer all rolled into one. The religious leaders of that day went to the Romans, who had taken Jesus prisoner, and made sure they would go before the people and give them the choice of releasing either Barabbas or Jesus...encouraging the crowd to choose Barabbas. When they had secured his release in the place of Jesus (see Matthew 27:15–26), Barabbas became a free man. So, too, by Jesus' death, we can become free men and women, because He took your place and mine under the curse of sin, sickness, and disease and paid the price with His very life.

It's important to notice that after Barabbas was released and Jesus took His place, no authority in Jerusalem could touch him for the crimes he had committed. His crimes had been forgiven him, or pardoned. In the same way, by Jesus' death on the Cross, our sins have been forgiven us; we've received a full pardon.

Jesus' sinless blood washed away your sins and set you free from the domination and oppressive affliction of the devil. And when you accept Christ as your Lord and Savior and the sacrifice He made for you on the Cross, the devil no longer has a legal right to touch you anymore. Just as Barabbas was physically set free, you have been set free spiritually from the wages of sin and death because of what Jesus has done. As Psalm 103:10–12 says,

>He has not dealt with us according to our sins, nor punished us according to our iniquities. For as the heavens are high above the earth, so great is His mercy toward those who fear Him; as far as the east is from the west, so far has He removed our transgressions from us.

To Live in You

The second reason Jesus died on the cross was so that He could live **in** you. Yes, it's true that He came to earth as flesh and blood, but His mission was beyond what any mere flesh and blood could ever have accomplished—to save as many as would believe on His name (John 1:12).

In order to accomplish this mission, Jesus needed to be omnipresent—present everywhere at the same time—which could not happen as long as He was on the earth in His bodily form, having taken on the physical limitations of a man. He had to die so that God could raise Him up in His Spirit form and He could live inside of you and me. Jesus is now omnipresent—meaning that He's present everywhere at the same time, always available to save those who accept Him as their Lord and Savior and to minister His healing and delivering power to those who reach out to Him in faith.

Listen to what Jesus said after His Resurrection when the disciples were worried because they knew Jesus would soon be leaving this earth to be with His Father in heaven. In John 14:16–18, He told them:

>I will pray the Father, and He will give you another Helper, that He may abide with you forever—the Spirit of truth, whom the world cannot receive, because it neither sees Him nor knows Him; but you know Him, for He

*dwells with you and **will be in you**. I will not leave you orphans; I will come to you.*

Jesus left this earth so that He could send the Holy Spirit to us to live **in** us forever. Jesus' resurrection brought the victory of good over evil. It signaled the breaking of the bondage of sin, sickness, disease, fear, doubt, and anything else that had stood between God and man. And now, according to Romans 8:11NLT, that same Spirit that raised Christ from the dead dwells in us, *and just as God raised Christ Jesus from the dead, he will give life to your mortal bodies by this same Spirit living within you.*

When Jesus died, He descended into hell and by virtue of His authority over all things, He broke the gates of hell and destroyed the devil's grip over mankind. He literally recaptured the dominion that God had originally given to Adam, but that Adam had given to Satan by default in the Garden of Eden through his sin and rebellion against God. Jesus restored mankind to his original status, which was elevated above Satan and all his demon forces.

Then having defeated Satan, death, hell, and the grave, Jesus' Spirit once again entered His lifeless body in the tomb so that on the third day He could be raised from the dead into newness of life. And having also set mankind free from sin, sickness, disease, and death, He says in Matthew 28:18 KJV, *all power is given unto me in heaven and in earth.*

By reason of Jesus' redemptive work on the Cross, healing, health, peace, and well-being now belong to every Christian, including *you*! **They are your rights**; Jesus earned them for you. Or perhaps a better way to say it is that they are your **benefits** for loving and serving Him.

Satan's Illegal Assaults

I believe it's very important for you to remember this any time you're fighting sickness or dis-ease in any area of your life:

if healing is your right as a born-again son or daughter of God, then that sickness or disease in your life is really trespassing where it doesn't belong. Sickness and disease have no legal right to indwell your body since Jesus destroyed their legal grounds more than two thousand years ago. He whose body knew no sickness was made to carry every sickness ever known to mankind when He hung on that Cross so that His healing power might come on you and me today.

What would you do if someone tried to come into your home illegally...a robber or a thief, or someone who was trying to deliver a package to you of some deadly thing that you did not want? You'd fight back! First, you'd claim legal right over the property that rightfully belonged to you, and then you'd command the trespasser to leave.

That's exactly what you need to do right now. If sickness or disease has tried to attach itself to you in any area of your life, it's time to exercise the legal rights Jesus has given you. It's time to violently command that sickness, that infirmity, that need—whatever it is—to come out of your life, and to take authority over it in Jesus' name.

Let's do that now. As your partner for miracles, I will add my faith to yours, as we take the authority Jesus gave us over every work of the devil that He came to destroy. As we take authority, let's declare God's word over your situation. Let's agree with what God has to say about your healing. Let's call things that are not as though they are, just as God does, according to Romans 4:17. Let's call you healed and whole by the power of the Holy Spirit living inside of you, the same Spirit that raised Christ from the dead. And let's command Satan to let go of God's property—you!

I encourage you to say these words out loud (or others, as you feel led) and let yourself hear God's Words coming out of your mouth. Let's pray right now:

> *Father, I thank You for the authority You've given me*
> *in the name of Jesus, the name that is above every name*

named in heaven and on earth. And right now, I speak to this _____ (specify whatever sickness, or disease, or difficulty you're facing, such as cancer, financial problems, etc.) and I command it to come out of my body, to let go of my life, and to go back to hell where it came from. Satan, you are illegally trespassing in my life, and I command you to take your hands off God's property, me. I belong to God, and according to Romans 8:11 the same Spirit that raised Jesus from the dead lives inside of me, and where the Spirit of God is, no sickness or disease or other evil, life-destroying thing can live. I declare that by Jesus' stripes, I am healed, according to Isaiah 53:5, and by the power of His Holy Spirit I am made whole. And according to Nahum 1:9, I command this evil thing not to rise up a second time. In Jesus' name, I pray. Amen.

Jesus tells us that when we have faith even as small as a mustard seed and we speak to our mountain of need—which you just did if you prayed that prayer—and do not doubt in our heart, but believe what we say will come to pass, then we can have *whatsoever we say.* (See Matthew 17:20 and Mark 11:23.)

Many people pray for healing and other needs, and once the prayer is over they begin immediately saying things like, "I wonder if that will work?" Or, "Well, I hope that makes a difference." Their words immediately negate what they just did; it's like planting a seed in the ground and then pouring gasoline on top of the seed so that it can never grow.

I want you to remember that your words are very important. *Death and life are in the power of the tongue,* Proverbs 18:21 tells us. We can literally speak words of life or words of death into our situation. I want to encourage you to continue to agree with God's Word, as we've just done, by speaking it over your circumstance as often as you need to until your miracle is complete. Remember my dad's explanation of "wenting," and how many healings happen over time. Don't get discouraged, and don't get into doubt by speaking words of death over your situation.

At the end of this book, I have included a list of positive, faith-building Scriptures that I believe can help you trust God for your miracle. And I encourage you to find other Scriptures that speak specifically to you, or about your situation, and add them to the list that you confess over your life. From experiences in my own life and ministry, and watching what has happened to so many people that write me or contact our ministry, I believe that practice can help you—perhaps more than any other—to receive the healing miracle you need. And I can't wait to hear from you when you do!

Chapter 6
MAKING ROOM FOR THE MIRACULOUS

In this chapter I want to talk to you about making room for the miraculous in your life.

I grew up seeing miracles. I grew up the son of a healing evangelist, watching my father pray for the sick and seeing many of those people healed by the power of God. It didn't matter what kind of problem they had—whether they had a physical problem that was medically incurable, a child that had suffered the effects of polio, or something as common as having warts on your hand, as I did as a child—I knew that you could pray and believe God for a miracle. In fact, I wouldn't even be alive if my father had not been miraculously healed of the advanced case of tuberculosis that was about to take his life as a young man.

At the age of 17, Dad was playing in a high school championship basketball game when he suddenly collapsed on the floor and had to be driven home. Doctors diagnosed him as having tuberculosis. For months after that, Dad lay on his bed, sick and literally hemorrhaging his life's blood out of his body day by day. By all earthly standards, he should have died just a few months later...and he came very close to death. But through the prayers and stubborn faith of my grandparents and other family members who loved my dad and believed in God's healing power—so much so that they picked him up and carried him to a man who was praying for the sick—the miracle-working power of God healed Oral Roberts and raised him off his death bed.

Earlier that day, on the way to the healing service he was taken to, the Lord had said to my dad, "Son I'm going to heal you and you're to take my healing power to your generation." The call to the miracle ministry of healing came upon my father that night just as God had said, as he was healed of not only the tuberculosis that had almost stolen his life, but also the terrible stuttering that had plagued him from his childhood. And if my father had not been healed of tuberculosis and had died as a teenager, I never would have been born. So it's fair to say that I owe my very life to a miracle. In fact, the very circumstances surrounding my birth were even miraculous.

My father was conducting a Healing Crusade in Dallas in November 1948. The last service was scheduled for the night of November 8. It had been a very powerful Crusade with many, many salvations and healings, and because of that the sponsoring pastors asked my father to extend the Crusade. "I'm sorry," he replied. "My wife Evelyn is expecting our third child tomorrow. Our first two children were born on the doctor's exact due date and I believe this one will be also, so I must go home tonight." The pastors said, "Brother Roberts, if you will extend the Crusade three more nights, so many more will be saved and healed. Couldn't you pray and ask your wife to postpone the baby three days?" It was an almost unbelievable request. But my dad understood what they were saying and felt the same way in his spirit, so he answered them, "Well, I guess I could call her."

Now when he reached my mother by phone, she was not too impressed with the new plan. Nevertheless, she said, "Oral, if you pray with me, I will agree with you in faith and ask the Lord to postpone the baby until the 12th ." You talk about faith! You talk about two people believing God…that surely is a phenomenal example of simply releasing your faith to God and trusting Him to perform a miracle.

The Crusade was extended, and many more people gave their hearts to the Lord, and many more healings occurred just as my dad and the sponsoring pastors had believed it would happen.

When it was over, Dad drove home to Tulsa late on November 11, and just as my parents had agreed in faith, I was born on November 12.

So my life literally began with a miracle. I have been around miracles and the miraculous power of God all of my life. Through the years, I have learned to **expect** God to perform miracles in my life, in my family, and in my ministry on a regular basis. And I have learned how to allow His Holy Spirit to operate through me, and how to recognize His operation through the lives of other people.

But I realize that many people did not grow up as I did. And many have not had the opportunity to witness miracles or to live in the kind of atmosphere of faith that I had. You may be one of those people. You may never have seen a miracle, or even heard of someone receiving a miracle, let alone experienced one in your life. I believe that as you read this book, that situation is going to change. I believe that as you open up your mind and your spirit to the possibility of miracles and begin to reach out to God, you will begin experiencing miracles for yourself. That's what I'm praying for you as you read this book. And that's why I want to talk to you about making room for the miraculous in your life.

Miracles Are Not Something Unusual with God

I've known people who believe that if there even is such a thing as a miracle, it must be something that only happens to a rare, few, privileged people…and it must be something that only happens in the most extreme circumstances.

But God's Word really does not support that explanation of miracles at all. In fact, from Genesis to Revelation, the overriding tone of the Bible is one of **miracles**…and of recognizing man's need for them on a daily basis.

Take the example of the Lord's Prayer, "Our father which art in heaven. Hallowed be thy name. Thy Kingdom come. They will be done in earth, as it is in heaven. And give us this day our **daily bread**…"

Our *daily* bread. God gives a supply for our needs in many different ways. He uses both natural and supernatural means. When the natural suffices, that is what God often gives us. But when the natural is insufficient, we can always turn to the all-sufficiency of God.

Our need in all the areas of our life is a daily need. And in expecting miracles every day, we begin to see the concern of a loving father over our lives.

I am deeply moved by this fact of God's nature. *I know He is concerned about my **daily** needs.* He is not just concerned about a need I may be facing in some extreme situation, although I know that He absolutely is concerned at those times…and certainly I turn to Him when I'm facing something extremely difficult or hurtful, for I know He is the God of the impossible. But even beyond that, *I know that God understands and is concerned about **everything** that touches my life on a daily basis.* And He stands ready to meet *every* need with His miracle-working power.

I have seen and experienced many miracles in my life and ministry, both in the natural and supernatural realms. And I know that a miracle has a supernatural effect in the physical world beyond the power of nature. It is wonderful and astonishing. And you just can't explain a miracle away.

Different Types of Miracles

There are many different types of miracles. One is a miracle that might happen to you or to me that we have been **expecting**.

Some time ago we received a call from a woman whose son had been critically injured in a car accident and had been paralyzed. After major surgery he was placed in the intensive care unit. The doctors told his mother, "It appears he will never walk again."

This woman told our Abundant Life Prayer Group prayer partner that she was *expecting a miracle* for her son's recovery and fully expected him to walk again and even play sports. Our prayer partner prayed and joined their faith with the woman's faith for a mighty miracle, and you know what... within a year that young man was completely healed by the power of God. **So expectant faith creates miracles.**

There can also be miracles that are **unexpected**. Some years ago I received a testimony of a man who found out firsthand that unexpected miracles happen.

He and his wife were scheduled to board a flight in Chicago when he got a feeling he should cancel out and make other travel plans...and he did just that. Later that day when the flight took off from Chicago's O'Hare airport, it crashed and many lives were lost. Now the man was not expecting a miracle that day when he canceled his plane flight. He was just following a feeling he had in his spirit. But it was truly a miracle that the man and his wife were not on that plane.

If you are praying about something, the Lord may give you a quickening inside—a feeling that you know something in the spirit realm that you could not have known in the natural realm. Through this quickening there will often be an answer to a problem or a situation. Then as you think back on this quickening you felt, you'll know in your heart that it was indeed a miracle and it cannot be explained away. (*I'll talk more about this special and supernatural way God sometimes communicates with us in the next chapter.*)

Then there is the miracle of an **extraordinary nature**, such as a complete change in your body, or your mind, or your circumstances. Someone who is instantly healed of any incurable disease, for instance, would fall into that category. And surely when we accept Jesus Christ as our personal Lord and Savior, there is a miracle of an extraordinary nature that takes place, as we become "new creatures in Christ" as 2 Corinthians 5:17 says, and our entire life begins to change.

A miracle may completely change someone close to you, sometimes even someone who has been an **enemy** to you. This happened to David in 1 Samuel 30:1–19 when an Egyptian from his enemy's camp showed him where the enemy was so that David could overtake them and recover all that had been stolen from him.

Often the force of the miracle that happens either inside of you or in someone else cannot be explained, except to say that it comes from the wonder-working power of a loving, healing, miracle-working God.

Only You Know

My soul, wait silently for God alone: for my expectation is from Him (Psalm 62:5).

Sometimes you're the only person who knows about a miracle that happens or is happening. You just know that you are very grateful to God for bringing it to pass.

In my life this happens quite often and I'm sure it happens in the lives of others too, for the Christian life is partially made up of such miracles. Take for example, an accident that is averted and you whisper in prayer, "Thank You, God. That was a miracle!"

Sometimes a miracle like that can change a person's life. Lindsay had something like that happen that put her into a new level of listening to and hearing from God. One day she was driving her car down Harvard Avenue here in Tulsa when she felt the Lord speak in her heart to stop at a certain store that was along her way. Well, Lindsay was busy and on her way to do something else so she said to the Lord very sincerely, "Okay, Lord, I'll stop by sometime later on." But the Lord kept impressing her to stop by that specific shop and to do it right away.

Lindsay couldn't imagine why she needed to stop there. Nevertheless, at the leading of the Lord she obeyed and made a brief stop in the shop that she felt God impressing on her heart. After a few minutes of looking around, waiting to see if there was something special she needed or perhaps someone she was supposed to meet there, she got back in her car and drove away. Just a few blocks down the road, as she turned back on to Harvard Avenue, she saw police cars and an ambulance stopped in the middle of the street. It was pretty obvious that a bad accident had taken place while she was in the store.

As Lindsay sat in her car in the line of traffic that was building up, she felt the Lord speaking to her again. This time He said to her, "I wasn't trying to get you to go in that shop. I was trying to save you from a very bad accident."

Now if Lindsay had kept on going down that street, she very well may have been involved in that serious car wreck. Who knows? She could have been badly hurt or even killed. But because she listened to the Lord and then obeyed, God kept her safe from danger.

Sometimes when things seem to be going wrong in your workplace, you can pray and often a change comes and you know you've just experienced a miracle. Tension is lifted, attitudes are improved, apologies are made, friendship is built, and things begin to get straightened out.

At home, a miracle can change the attitude of one family member toward another, and suddenly everybody seems to be getting along better. I have known of children who believed that miracles would happen to one or both of their parents, such as deliverance from alcoholism or drug addiction, and then miracles did happen. I have known parents who believed for miracles in their children and have seen tremendous results from the Lord because they did.

I'll never forget a pastor who had almost lost his ministry because of the delinquency of his children. He told me that every time he stood up to preach, his "failure" with his son was almost like a physical blow. Even though he had taught his son the difference between right and wrong and had been a good example to him, and even though he loved his son...for some reason the young man had gone away from the teachings of his childhood and broken his father's heart.

This pastor said to me, "Richard, I believed every day that my son would come back home and turn away from the temptation he had been following. Every morning when I awakened, I would say, 'Lord, today may be the day.'" And that day finally did come! Today that son pastors a great church and is highly respected in his community. Why? I believe the expectant spirit of a father's faith for a miracle in his son's life brought this miracle to pass.

Even when I personally ran from God, it was my mother who said to me, "Son, you will never get away from my prayers." She held on to the faith rope of prayer and expectation for me and would not turn loose. And the great day finally came when I fell on my knees at 19 years of age, put my head in her lap as I'd done when I was just a little boy, and fully committed my life to Christ. I know that it was the prayers and expectant faith of my parents that brought me to God.

Expecting Is the Beginning

Therefore I say to you, whatever things you ask when you pray, believe that you receive them, and you will have them (Mark 11:24).

Parents who have sick children often bring about their child's healing through their expectant attitude: "Today could be the day God heals my child."

My grandparents, Ellis and Claudius Roberts, held onto their faith for my father's healing from tuberculosis even when so many other people had all but given up hope. One day my grandmother had to go to the grocery store. Everyone there knew her and knew how desperate the situation was. When she walked into the store it was obvious that she was in tears. One of the store clerks said, "Oh, Mrs. Roberts, has Oral died?"

"Oh no," she replied, "Why do you ask that?"

"I saw you crying," he said.

She said, "I'm not crying because I'm sad, but because I'm happy."

"What do you mean?" he asked.

To that, my grandmother answered, "I believe that God is going to heal my son and someday he will preach the Gospel!" she replied.

What faith! What expectation!

I have often wondered how much of my father's healing can be traced back to the expectant faith of my grandparents, for their expectancy increased day by day until it reached a climax and my dad was healed.

Expectancy is like that. It creates an atmosphere for deliverance and sets the stage for a miracle. It gets people in the right frame of mind. I believe it influences heaven and starts things happening.

My father's healing from tuberculosis was no fluke. It happened not only through God's love and concern for him, but also because of the expectant faith of his parents.

When sickness strikes or whenever there is some kind of satanic attack against you, it is good to surround yourself with people who believe in the healing power of a caring God and who make room for the miraculous in their lives. You may say, "Richard, I don't know anyone like that." Well, in that case it may be time for you to rethink some of your old associations and consider letting God lead you to some new ones.

My grandparents would not allow anyone into my dad's room who would only add a negative element to the atmosphere and who would not go into a faith agreement for his healing.

One day my aunt Jewel came into the room and said seven words that changed my father's life forever.

"Oral, God is going to heal you," Jewel said to her little brother.

"Is he, Jewel?" my dad honestly responded.

"Yes!" was her strong reply.

Then one day not long after that, my Uncle Elmer came for my dad and said, "Oral, there's a man holding healing services in a tent in town, and people are getting healed every night. I'm going to drive you there and take you to be prayed for."

You see, it was the *expectant* faith in the people who surrounded my father that stirred his own *dormant* faith to believe that, although he had been bedfast for five months, and although the doctors were not having any success with the medicines, he could actually receive a miracle touch from God and be healed.

And as that man of God layed his hands on Dad that night before a large crowd, my father **was** healed. In a moment's time, the tuberculosis was literally driven out of his body and he could breathe all the way down. And for extra measure, God also healed the stuttering that had plagued my dad all his life. What his family and those who loved him were all expecting... actually happened!

I remember several years ago praying for a little child who was very sick, and had been sick for a long time. His mother said to me, "Richard, I just know that God is going to heal my son." "How do you know?" I asked. "Believe me," she replied, "I just know." And as we prayed, it happened just as she expected it to.

It Happens Over and Over

Through the years, I have seen this happen so many times and in so many different ways I could never count them all. In my ministry, I constantly receive letters and e-mail from people telling me that expecting a miracle caused them to find the best job they ever had, or caused their business to change dramatically for the better, or caused some other miracle to come into their lives.

Not long ago I received a testimony through our Abundant Life Prayer Group from a man who had tried to get a job at a particular company for several years. He wanted to work there because it was close to his home and it paid good wages. Time and again he had applied and checked on his application, but for some unknown reason he couldn't get the job.

One night he was watching me on TV. I was talking about planting a seed of faith and expecting miracles. That night he called to plant a financial seed into our ministry and released his faith for the job of his dreams to finally come through. The next day he telephoned again to say that this time the company had called to offer him the job, and he had accepted it.

Open Up to the Possibility of Miracles

Testimonies like this, and many others like it, encourage me to keep urging people to *make room for the miraculous* in their lives...and to begin to really **expect** miracles from the Lord. I tell you, God is so *good*, and He wants to prosper you in every area of your life (3 John 2). He wants to heal you. He wants you to enter into the fullness of His Holy Spirit. God wants your life to count for His kingdom, and He has only *good* plans for your future (Jeremiah 29:11).

You are important to God. He did not make you to be a nobody. *He made you to be a somebody.* And He has a unique place for you in this world and a purpose that only you can fulfill.

More than anything, I want to see you healed and whole so that you can continue to live out the life God has planned for you...and continue to touch the lives of so many others that He has put in your path. It's hard to do that as well as you would like to when you're sick, isn't it? Or living in a financial mess that can make you feel like you're bound up in a straight-jacket...or dealing with any of a number of the life-restricting schemes that the devil has brought against you.

Sometimes our miracle is as close as a single word from the Lord that He longs to whisper to our hearts, for as I've heard it said many times, "one word from the Lord can change your life forever." But when life throws us such death-dealing blows as you may be going through right now, it's sometimes hard to hear Him communicating with us. I understand. I've been there, too.

I believe it's very important to stay sensitive to the Lord and ready to obey every word of instruction He speaks. I thank God for the *logos*—the written Word of God in the Bible. How would we know anything about God's character and His will for our lives without it? But I also thank God for the *rhema*—that personal and intimate word that He speaks to each one of us in our day-to-day relationship with Him, as our Father, our Friend, and the One who can guide us safely through the minefield of this life until we meet Him in heaven some day.

In the next chapter, I want to talk to you about the most faithful Friend you could ever have. The One who lives inside of you, if you have accepted Christ as your Lord and Savior, and who longs to talk to you and have you talk back to Him, in the way any loving Father would with His beloved child. God has given each of us a personal, and supernatural, way we can do that…any time and any place when we're open and sensitive to His leading.

First, let's join our faith together, and believe God for the miraculous to begin opening up more and more in your life every day.

Father, You were a miracle-working God in the Bible… and I believe You still are today. If You ever performed any miracles, You're still performing them today…if You ever healed anyone, You're still healing people today…because You don't change and You show no partiality to Your children.

Right now, I open myself up to Your supernatural power in a new way, and I make room for the miraculous in my life, as I begin to truly expect miracles from You. Thank You for Your saving, healing, delivering power…and right now I receive that miracle-working power into my life. In Jesus' name, Amen.

Chapter 7

A WONDERFUL AND SUPERNATURAL WAY TO PRAY

Likewise the Spirit also helps in our weaknesses. For we do not know what we should pray for as we ought, but the Spirit Himself makes intercession for us with groanings which cannot be uttered (Romans 8:26).

Letting the Holy Spirit Help You in Your Situation

When you were born again and accepted Jesus as your personal Lord and Savior, the Holy Spirit came inside of your spirit and bore witness with you that you were now indeed a child of God. That's what Scripture tells us in Romans 8:16. So if you are a born-again Christian, you have the Holy Spirit living inside of you. There's no other way that you could have received Christ except by the power of the Holy Spirit working in you.

And because you do have the Holy Spirit living in you, I have wonderful news that I believe can help you in your day-to-day relationship with God, especially in praying and talking to Him and hearing back from Him. God has provided a wonderful and supernatural way to pray—a *prayer language*—for every believer in Jesus. It's sometimes called "the baptism of the Holy Spirit," or "praying in the Spirit," or "praying in your personal prayer language," or sometimes it's referred to as "praying in tongues." However, this is not the same as the *gift of tongues* that the Apostle Paul referred to in 1 Corinthians 12:8–10, when he was describing the nine gifts of the Spirit that are completely at the discretion of the Holy Spirit to disperse whenever and wherever He wills.

No, this "prayer language" is something that every born-again Christian has access to, once you have received Jesus as your Lord.

Now, there's been a lot of misunderstanding about this among believers. And I'm sorry to say that we Pentecostals and Charismatics have sometimes gotten it wrong in the past. At times we have even hurt and confused other believers by saying things like, "when did you receive the Holy Spirit?" when what we meant to ask was "when did you begin praying in the Spirit?" Because all of us received the Holy Spirit the minute we accepted Jesus into our hearts. And we don't have to have some other experience or go out and "get" Someone that we already have. It's very clear in 1 Corinthians 12:3 that *no one can say that Jesus is Lord except by the Holy Spirit.*

We have accidentally intimidated some of our fellow believers into thinking that they are somehow "less than" we are because they don't pray in the Spirit. But the real truth of the matter is that I don't pray in tongues because I'm *better* than anyone else—and neither does any other Christian—but because I need help and guidance to know how to better live my life.

So I want you to understand that it is not a requirement to pray in tongues to go to heaven. And it's not a badge that you wear, saying, "Look at me. Look at how important I am. I speak in tongues." That is not the measuring stick. The measuring stick is, "Whosoever shall call upon the name of the Lord shall be saved."

We're not special or somehow more spiritual because we pray in tongues. In fact, it's exactly the opposite. I pray in tongues because I don't always know *how* to pray or *what* I even need to pray *for*. *I pray in tongues because I need help.* Often I don't know what to do, I don't know what to say, I don't know how to pray in the way that would be most fruitful, as Paul said in Romans 8:26. Without praying in the Spirit and getting God's response back to me, I don't know how to live my life in the way God wants me to.

Let me give you just one small example of what I'm talking about. Many times when I am overseas in foreign nations conducting Healing Crusades—praying for tens of thousands of people and facing things that I don't face in my day-to-day life—I don't exactly know how to handle situations that may come up. So I pray in tongues, and then I pray in English, and God will give me understanding. Suddenly, I just know what to do. So I don't pray in tongues because I'm smarter or better than anybody else. I pray in tongues because I need God's supernatural help. I can't figure out everything I need to know, or do everything I need to do in my own human flesh and understanding alone.

Every born-again believer can pray in tongues, or in their prayer language. It's simply a decision of your will. I'm not saying that you *have to*, but I am saying that you *can*. And the prayer language that the Holy Spirit gives you can give you the ability to talk to and hear from God in a new way...a way you never dreamed possible before.

Back to the Way God Intended

The Bible tells us that God created man with the ability to *respond to* Him and to *know* Him. In Genesis we're told that God walked and talked with Adam and Eve in the Garden, in the cool of the day. However, it wasn't long before they broke that original relationship with God. And how did they break it? By sin…by disobeying God's law that He had put in place for their protection. God told Adam and Eve that they could eat from any tree in the Garden, but they were not to eat from the tree of the knowledge of good and evil. And when they disobeyed God and broke that relationship with Him, they died *spiritually.*

Remember that Satan, in the form of a snake, had told Adam and Eve, "God said to you that if you eat of the tree of the knowledge of good and evil, you shall surely die."

But then Satan did what he is still doing to us today. He took a Scripture and perverted it. He told Eve, "God said you'll die…but you're not really going to die. He knows that when you eat of that tree, you will become like a god yourself." And he tempted them to disobey God. Well, as usual, he was half right and half wrong. Adam and Eve weren't going to die *physically* when they disobeyed God, but there was going to be a *spiritual* death. And when they committed sin, they broke the contract or the covenant they had enjoyed with God, and they died spiritually. They didn't die physically at that point, but they died *spiritually. And they lost their ability to communicate with God in the personal, intimate way they had always known before.*

That spiritual death has been passed on to all of Adam and Eve's descendants, and that includes us. All of us were born with a "sin nature" or a leaning toward sin. That's why we need a Redeemer.

The very innermost part of us is called our spirit. In the original Greek, the word is pneuma. And your spirit, or your pneuma, was created for one main purpose. It's very simple: to know God. That's why you were created. You were created to know God.

Adam and Eve *knew* God. And when you're born again, the Holy Spirit comes back into your spirit to restore that original relationship with God that Adam and Eve had in the Garden. He brings you the ability to reestablish that original communication with your heavenly Father, so that it's no longer fractured or broken.

When man chose to disobey God by nourishing his mind over nourishing his spirit—or, in other words, choosing to eat of the tree of the knowledge of good and evil, rather than choosing to eat of the tree of life which God had told them they could do—he elevated his soul over his spirit. And through the new birth experience, we can begin again to relate to God through our spirits…to live from our spirit first.

We Need the Holy Spirit's Power

In Acts, chapter 2, we're told the account of the outpouring of the Holy Spirit, after Jesus had been resurrected and ascended to His Father in heaven. As I talked about in an earlier chapter, Jesus had promised the disciples that He would not leave them alone and comfortless when He left this earth…that He would send them His Holy Spirit to live inside of them (John 14:16–18). But now, in Acts 1:8—just moments before He was taken up into heaven—He told them something very specific about what the Holy Spirit would do in their lives. He said to them, *You shall receive power when the Holy Spirit has come upon you.*

He promised them *power*…the power to lives their lives in a victorious way, and even to have the strength and courage to be His witnesses. To a frightened, ragtag group of disciples that had not long before fled into hiding so that no one would know they were Jesus' associates, He gave the responsibility of being His "witnesses," of telling the world about Him and building His church until even the gates of hell would not prevail against it.

As you read the Book of Acts and the rest of the New Testament, you can see that that's exactly what the disciples did. On the Day of Pentecost, when the Holy Spirit was poured out for the first time, a holy boldness came upon them like they had never known before. They came out of hiding and began preaching and proclaiming the wonderful works of God in the streets, among great crowds of people...and they did it in heavenly languages—languages that were not necessarily known to them. But those in the crowd understood what they were saying and heard them speaking the wonderful works of God in their own languages. On that first day alone, we're told in Acts 2:41 that 3,000 people accepted the message of the Gospel and were saved. And we're told further in verse 43 that *many wonders and signs were done through the faith and prayers of the apostles.*

Now, some people believe that the Holy Spirit coming upon people was a one-time event, meant for the Book of Acts days only. Maybe they believe that you and I today don't need the power of the Holy Spirit working in our lives in the same way that the apostles and those in the early Church needed it. But I believe that we need the Holy Spirit's help every bit as much today, if not more so.

The Holy Spirit Helps Our Weaknesses

I believe that prayer is one of the most important tools that God has given us to live a victorious life. In fact, the Bible tells us that we should *pray always* (Ephesians 6:18). What is prayer? It is simply talking to God and listening for Him to talk back to you. Sounds simple, doesn't it? But, if you're like me, you've probably found that sometimes it's more difficult than it sounds. At times it seems you can't even find the right words. Problems may be flooding through your mind, and you want to tell God how you feel, but you don't know how. And it seems that often the cares of this world—some of the very cares you may be facing right now—can try to choke out God's voice, until we may barely be able to hear what He is saying to us.

The good news is that God has given us a way that we can talk to Him when the words just don't seem to come. That's what Romans 8:26–27 is talking about when it says: *The Spirit also helps in our weaknesses. For we do not know what we should pray for as we ought, but the Spirit Himself makes intercession for us with groanings which cannot be uttered.* When we don't know how to pray about something that's bothering us, or something that we want to hear from God about, we can talk to God in a language that we've never learned before—just as the disciples did on the Day of Pentecost. Through the power of the Holy Spirit, we can pray in a "heavenly language," a prayer language of the Spirit, a supernatural way to pray...and through it we can be in perfect communication with God just as Adam and Eve were when they walked and talked with God in the Garden.

Now praying in a prayer language isn't something to be afraid of, or something that makes you weird, or something that's on the fringes of Christianity. Most people who know me know that I would never participate in, or encourage *you* to participate in, something that isn't based on the Word of God. No, this is something that is very, very *powerful* in a Christian's life.

You may be saying to yourself right now, "Hey, wait a minute! How does this apply to me? I'm a Presbyterian...or I'm a Church of God member...or I'm a Baptist...or a Catholic...or an Assemblies of God member"...or whatever other denomination or group you belong to. The wonderful thing about this supernatural way to pray is that it's for *everybody*, no matter what label you're wearing.

The Holy Spirit came into your spirit on the day you accepted Christ and turned your life over to Him. He's been there ever since. Sometimes people have the mistaken idea that "receiving the Holy Spirit" is a separate experience from salvation. They may believe, or may have been incorrectly taught, that you have to wait until you're somehow "spiritual enough" to do that.

But according to the Word of God, we don't have to wait for anything, because there's no reason to try and "go out and get" something—or *Someone*—that you already have.

Jesus said in John 7:38–39, *"He who believes in Me, as the Scripture said, 'From his innermost being will flow rivers of living water.'" But this He spoke of the Spirit, whom those who believed in Him were to receive.*

Praying in the Spirit—or in your prayer language—is a decision that each of us can make by an act of our human will. And if we only understood it, we could have released our prayer language the very moment of our salvation, as the Holy Spirit was bearing witness with our spirit that we were indeed a child of God. Often it happens at a later time simply because we've not been taught that it's possible.

But whenever we do it, it is a decision of our will. **It is an experience that is under our control**. Paul said in 1 Corinthians 14:15, *I **will** pray with the spirit, and I **will** also pray with the understanding.* "I will" in this passage can be interpreted to mean "I determine to" or "I decide to."

Now this experience is not what Paul describes in 1 Corinthians 12:8–10 as the "gift of tongues." All of the nine gifts of the Spirit listed in that passage are completely under the control and at the discretion of the Holy Spirit to manifest through whomever He wills, and they are generally manifested in and for a group of people. A "gift of tongues" only flows through a believer as the Holy Spirit wills; it is not something that is subject to our control (only in that we can always *refuse to receive* the operation of any of the gifts of the Holy Spirit in our lives; but believe me, that is not something you want to do).

I think this is another area where many people are confused. Praying in a prayer language that the Holy Spirit gives to you alone is something that you can use every day in your own personal devotions and time of prayer. Whereas a gift of the Spirit is generally used in a corporate or group setting and is intended for the benefit of *other people*, praying in the Spirit is to benefit *you*... to build you up and edify *you*.

That's one reason I'm so interested right now in your beginning to pray in the Spirit if you've never done it before, or beginning to pray in the Spirit on a more regular basis if you've only done it on occasion. At this time in your life, when you're facing a need for healing in some important area of your life, I want you to have every resource available from the Lord that can help you *in* your weaknesses, and that can help you *overcome* those weaknesses. I believe that praying in the Spirit is one of the best tools God has given us for that purpose. The more we stay sensitive to His voice in prayer, the more God can minister healing to us in a much more personal and intense way...in more of a whole-person kind of way.

Jude 1:20 AMP encourages us to *build yourselves up [founded] on your most holy faith [make progress, rise like an edifice higher and higher], praying in the Holy Spirit.* Because we are not just a body only, but body, mind, and spirit, I believe it's very possible that as our spirit-man grows and is strengthened, our body and our mind—the areas where we struggle with most of our dis-ease—can be strengthened as well.

So while we don't *have* to pray in the Spirit, or in tongues, it's something that I strongly encourage you to do. It has made all the difference in my own life and in Lindsay's life, especially in times when we were hurting so badly it seemed like the pain would never stop.

When Your Whole World Falls Apart

Many years ago when Lindsay and I were first married, we wanted to have a child. We knew that we would have a difficult time because Lindsay had been told as a young woman that she had a physical condition which would most likely prevent her from ever having children. But in spite of that, we believed that God would give us the desires of our heart, and our desire was to have children.

For several years we struggled with Lindsay's physical problems: she would have difficulty becoming pregnant, then when she conceived she would not be able to carry the child to full term and she would miscarry. She also faced surgeries that could have put an end to any hope of having children. We went through disappointment after disappointment.

Then a miracle happened: Lindsay became pregnant and was able to carry the baby the full nine months. We were so thrilled! The pregnancy went well and the day finally came when Lindsay gave birth to a beautiful baby boy...a baby that *appeared* to be healthy when he was first born.

But within a matter of a few hours, it became apparent that he wasn't healthy. Something was very seriously wrong with our son. And as we stayed at the hospital, waiting and hoping and praying, we watched helplessly as our little boy died just 36 hours after he had come into this world.

As anyone who has ever lost a child can understand, Lindsay and I were completely devastated. After waiting so long for a child, to lose him that way—that quickly, and in spite of all the prayer that was being prayed for him—was almost beyond our comprehension.

The devil taunted us by telling us things like, you've prayed for others to be healed, yet you couldn't keep your own child alive. Our hearts were broken in a way we had never known before, and in a way that we realized some people never recover from.

Lindsay was especially torn apart emotionally. I had been scheduled to leave the United States for a Healing Crusade in

Africa not long after the baby's birth date. As I traveled and ministered, Lindsay planned to be at home with the baby. She knew she would miss me, of course, but she also knew that she would be extremely busy taking care of our son...and was she ever looking forward to that! To finally have a child to love and care for was the deepest desire of her heart.

Now her heart and her emotions were shattered into a million pieces. Not only did she not have the baby to love and care for, I was leaving her alone to go to a part of the world where we couldn't even communicate with each other like you would be able to do now with cell phones and Internet connections.

It was hard for us to make the decision that had to be made. But we both felt it was very important for me to keep the commitment I had made to go to Nigeria.

All Lindsay and I could do at this point was to pour out our hearts to God and ask Him to pour out His healing power into our lives. Many times as we held each other, we would pray in the Spirit together, allowing the Holy Spirit to pray through us when we couldn't put words to the pain that we were feeling, and to comfort us in the way that only He could do.

After we had been praying in our prayer language together, Lindsay told me one day that she believed the Lord was telling her that she was supposed to go with me to Nigeria. It was obviously not something that either of us had planned for, so travel arrangements still had to be made for her to go. I had to leave before that could be accomplished, so we made plans to meet in Nigeria as soon as Lindsay could get there.

I know how hard it must have been for her to get on that airplane that day...with a broken heart...and a physical body still reeling from the effects of recently having given birth. But both of us believed that, somehow, this must be a part of the answer for us to be able to get over what had just happened to us in the loss of our child. We knew this was God's leading, not our own.

Later when Lindsay arrived, we learned that Nigeria had one of the highest infant mortality rates in the world. So we were in a place where many people were dealing with the same kind of pain and hurting that Lindsay and I were dealing with. In God's wisdom, He had given us the opportunity to give out of our own pain into the lives of other people...to plant seeds of faith for our own healing, by loving and praying for their needs so that the harvest might come back into our lives—or as James 5:16 says it, *to pray for one another, that **you** may be healed.*

Lindsay and I will never forget that time in our lives—that incredible trip to Nigeria, the many healings that we saw among the precious Nigerian people...and how God used that time to begin to heal our broken hearts. After the birth of our son, we were afraid to think of ever trying to have another child...Lindsay especially. But as God ministered to us day by day in our times of praying together in the Spirit and allowing Him to communicate His healing love to us, we were able to try again to have a baby. The next year, our oldest daughter, Jordan—who is now a college graduate and an integral part of our ministry—was born. And later God blessed us with two more daughters, as well, Olivia and Chloe, who have also been the joy of our lives.

Right now, as you're suffering with a physical or emotional illness, or whatever you're dealing with specifically, you might say, "Richard, you just don't understand what I'm going through."

I once heard someone say that "pain is pain, no matter how it comes. It hurts to be hurt." And I believe that. I don't know if Lindsay and I would ever have been able to deal with the pain and disappointment of losing our son if it had not been for the healing power of God that came to us as we prayed together in the Spirit and tried to stay sensitive to what God was saying back to us in return. Having lived through the pain of losing a child, and many others things that are not often known publicly, I understand what it feels like when you hurt so bad you wonder if you'll be able to make it through.

But even if I don't understand what your situation is like, or how desperate you are to be healed, be assured that there's Someone who *does* understand it. His name is Jesus, and He has the *power* to set you free.

I've often heard my dad say, "God is big enough to take whatever we throw at Him. And He doesn't hold it against us when we tell Him how we feel." So share your feelings and your frustrations with Him. Tell Him how you *really* feel; not the polite words we all sometimes use in answer to a well-meaning question of, "How are you today?" God knows your true feelings anyway, whether you voice them to Him or not. And in His own Word, He's telling you to cast—or to **throw**—all of your worries and cares on Him so that He can carry them for you...*for He cares for you affectionately and cares about you watchfully* (1 Peter 5:7 AMP).

Since the day you accepted Christ, the Holy Spirit has been inside of you interceding to the Father in your behalf. He is not only searching your heart, but He is praying what I like to call a "straight-line" prayer to the Father. As Romans 8:27 AMP says, *He Who searches the hearts of men knows what is in the mind of the [Holy] Spirit [what His intent is], because the Spirit intercedes and pleads [before God] in behalf of the saints according to and in harmony with God's will.*

Through praying in your heavenly prayer language, you have the opportunity to enter into that **perfect** prayer. In other words, while you and I pray with our limited understanding and ability to communicate—or as we "beat around the bush," you could say, with God—the Holy Spirit is *praying exactly* what the problem is and *receiving exactly* what the answer is back from the Father.

Who wouldn't want to do that?

In 1 Corinthians 14:13, Paul also tells us, *Let him who prays in an unknown tongue pray that he may* **interpret**. While it's true that our *spirit* may be edified and lifted up just by praying in our prayer language, our *mind* doesn't have a clue what's going on. So in order to understand what the answer is that's coming back from God, we need to ask God to let us have an "interpretation" of our prayer.

By that I don't mean a word-for-word interpretation, but a sense of what God's response to us is. That's why Paul said in verse 15 of that same chapter, *I will pray with my spirit [by the Holy Spirit that is within me], but I will also pray [intelligently] with my mind and understanding* (Amplified version). When we pray in the Spirit, we can pray that God will "water" or illuminate our mind so that we can understand His response back to us and what He's saying to us or telling us to do.

When I pray in the Spirit and then stop and pray in English, usually one of two things happens. I either begin to say in English what I've been trying to say to the Lord but was unable to express before, or I get God's response back to me. Many times I begin to get direction from the Lord about something I need to do in my life, or He may give me insight into what I need to do about a certain situation that I wouldn't have known what to do about otherwise.

No matter what happens, after praying in the Spirit, and then praying in my own language with understanding, I am edified in my inner man in a way that I'm not sure anything else can do. I am built up in my faith and I believe that my entire person— spirit, soul, and body—receives a type of Holy Spirit "therapy." It's wonderful. It's one of the greatest abilities God has given to us to use in our everyday life.

I Want to Help You Release This Wonderful Experience

I've had the privilege of helping many people release the prayer language of the Spirit in their lives, and I'm glad to have this opportunity to help **you** right now. As we've talked about so many times, the Holy Spirit—the third person of the Holy Trinity—is inside of you as a born-again believer. There's no question about that. And God has always been a speaking God. He wants to speak to you and through you in this wonderful prayer language that can help you express everything you would like to express to Him, but your mind—limited as it is—may not be able to express in human language alone.

If you're ready to pray in the Spirit, I would first of all encourage you to begin to worship the Lord in your own earthly language— the language you already know. Just focus your mind on Jesus. Shut out everything else around you and just begin to worship Him. Tell Him how wonderful He is, how much you love Him.

Jesus said in John 7:38 NASB, *"He who believes in Me, as the Scripture said, 'From his innermost being will flow rivers of living water.'"* As you continue to worship God, you'll begin to feel that living water—the power of God…the Holy Spirit—coming up in your spirit. You've probably felt Him many times before, but didn't know what to do. This time when you feel Him building in your spirit, just open your mouth and let whatever supernatural words or syllables that seem to form come up and out over your tongue.

Many people receive only a few syllables, or sounds, at first, like I did, and they may not make any sense to you at all. In fact they will probably sound very strange to your ears. That's because this is a *heavenly* language, not an earthly language like the one you're used to speaking that originates in your mind.

Don't worry about how you feel or what anyone else may think. Just allow those new words and syllables to come out. Speak them out loud so your ears can hear them. I believe your faith will be built up as you hear yourself speaking a language that you know you're not forming with your mind, but that is coming directly out of your spirit to God.

After a little while, when you feel more comfortable praying in the Spirit, begin to pray in your earthly language again. Just say the first words that come to your mind, and then expect the Lord to give you insight and understanding as you continue to pray, first in the Spirit and then with your understanding again. You may hear yourself declaring the wonderful works of God, or you may begin hearing God's response back to your prayer to Him.

I do this every day, many times a day. You can do it anywhere, very quietly under your breath, and I do that. As I've continued to pray in the Spirit over the years, I have learned how to hear God's response back to me and to use the insight He gives me to live my daily life—whether for simple, everyday events and problems that occur, or for the more serious times of desperation. There are times when I know I must speak to Him and know that He is speaking directly back to me and ministering His healing power to my life—as the time I told you about when we lost our firstborn son years ago. That kind of loving, healing ministry of the Holy Spirit may be something you need desperately right now.

I can't encourage you strongly enough to begin to pray in the Spirit on a regular basis. Jude 1:20–21 says, *Beloved,* [build] *yourselves up on your most holy faith, praying in the Holy Spirit, keep yourselves in the love of God, looking for the mercy of our Lord Jesus Christ unto eternal life.*

I believe you'll find it tremendously helpful, as I do, in building up your faith to give you the power and direction you need to live every day. You may hear a word from God, or you may feel Him giving you insight into something that can help bring healing into your life—for your spirit, your mind, and your body. For as I said earlier, one word from God can change your life forever.

In the next chapter, I want to talk to you about the importance of agreeing with God's Word in order to "pull down" from heaven those things you need for your total healing.

Chapter 8

PULLING DOWN THE MIRACLE YOU NEED FROM HEAVEN

All of us have areas of need in our lives…areas where we need to hear from the Lord, either for something that *we* need from Him, or to know what He is wanting from us or wanting us to do next.

Sometimes those words from the Lord come directly from Him to us. Sometimes, we can hear Him speaking to us through other people, often through one of the gifts of the Spirit talked about in 1 Corinthians 12:8–10. But however God communicates with us, we have to learn to become sensitive to His Holy Spirit's leading in our lives so that we don't miss something very important He is trying to tell us, and so we know how to respond to and obey Him in whatever area He is leading.

For instance, in the last year, many people have come to me with different "words" of prophecy for me and for my ministry. I always feel that it's important to listen to words that come to you like that, especially when you know the credibility of the person involved.

One person who I really respect told me that when I turned 60 years old I would step into a whole new level of anointing—or God's presence and power—in my ministry.

I believed what the person was telling me. I knew they were a very credible person in the body of Christ. And I wanted that to be true of my ministry. I longed to step into the next level of anointing that God has for me.

But how was I supposed to make sure that was accomplished? Should I have said, "Thank you," and then just sat in a chair for several months, waiting for that word of prophecy to come to pass in my life.

No. If I had done that, I truly believe that I might never have experienced that new anointing, and never begun to see more people healed than ever before in my ministry. I began to "pull down" that word for my life by confessing it out loud every day.

I would say, "God's new anointing is coming upon me. I am sensitive to the Holy Spirit's moving in my life, and I immediately obey what He tells me to do." Then I would look for opportunities to minister to people or to pray for them and give that anointing a chance to begin operating in my life. I would "practice" walking in that anointing, day in and day out, until it became like a second nature to me. And since I turned 60, I can honestly say that God's anointing on me has been stronger than I've ever seen it in my life. When I minister, I've begun to feel His presence on me in a stronger and stronger way, and I've begun to experience unprecedented miracles everywhere I go.

As I've told you earlier in this book, God wants us to be participants with Him in living the abundant life He came to bring us. God will not do everything for us. He wants us to grow up and take on the responsibility for becoming mature men and women in Him. In addition to that, we know that we have an enemy of our soul, Satan, who wants to stop God's kingdom from growing and prospering in this world...and keep you, and all believers, from experiencing all the wonderful benefits that are rightfully ours as children of the King. And our enemy is not shy; he's very active in his pursuits, as 1 Peter 5:8 describes when it warns us, *Be sober, be vigilant; because your adversary the devil walks about like a roaring lion, seeking whom he may devour.*

So we know there's a battle raging in the kingdom of God. We can't afford to sit idly by and let the enemy reign over us, or cheat us out of what God has prepared for us from the foundation of the world.

Matthew 11:12 says, *The kingdom of heaven suffers violence, and the violent take it by force.* The Amplified version spells it out even more clearly than that, when it says, *The kingdom of heaven has endured violent assault, and violent men seize it by force [as a precious prize—a share in the heavenly kingdom is sought with most ardent zeal and intense exertion].*

Many times when I pray for groups of people, God may give me a word of knowledge that seems to apply to a specific person in the crowd. And often that person will stand up and tell me that he or she was the one who had been suffering from the particular problem I mentioned, and is now healed. But often as not, there are *many* people who hook their faith onto the words God gives me and begin to "claim" that healing miracle for themselves. And they're healed just the same.

For instance, I may have a word of knowledge that God is healing someone who has a breathing problem. But someone with some other kind of problem, perhaps in their chest rather than just their lungs, takes a leap of faith and claims the healing for their own. Or sometimes it may be 10 people...or 20 people. It doesn't seem to matter. What matters is that they are reaching out with their faith and "seizing their miracle by force" as Matthew 11:12 indicates that we need to do. And often those same people are healed.

Once in a service, I gave a word of knowledge about someone's back being healed and 500 people testified of receiving healing. Now that's truly amazing, isn't it!

Healing of HIV/AIDS

I want to share a wonderful healing report that we just received not long ago in our ministry. It's a healing from one of the most deadly and feared diseases known to man…and one that millions of people have died from worldwide—HIV/AIDS.

An associate of mine in our ministry first learned of this healing. His parents live next door to a man named John who is originally from Kenya. John lives in Texas now and over a period of time, I have come to know him. John heard that we had been invited to Kenya to talk to government leaders and meet with some of the leading pastors there about conducting a Healing Crusade. We also planned to bring in a medical team and a team of people to provide nutritious meals for those who were starving. John talked to us about the possibility of going with us on the trip, and I agreed.

What I didn't know was that John's wife had an aunt living in Kenya who had HIV/AIDS. She had had it for several years and was on medication to treat it but, of course, at this time there still is no known cure for HIV/AIDS.

The woman had boils and lesions on her body. She was always very tired, and in between her doctor visits and treatments she had to sleep and rest a lot of the time. She also had terrible headaches and she suffered from them constantly. As the mother of three children, college and high-school age, she'd had to hire someone to help her with daily chores such as doing laundry and preparing meals because in her illness she couldn't keep up with the demands of a busy household.

The good news was that John's aunt-in-law was a believer in Jesus, and though she had HIV/AIDS, she never wavered from believing that God would heal her. John had talked to her on the phone many times, but had never met his wife's aunt. He had told her that we were soon coming to Kenya and had encouraged her, still completely unknown to me, to come to one of the services where we would be ministering.

The night before we arrived in Kenya, the woman had a dream. In her dream, she saw what looked like a huge group of Kenyans in a service of some kind, along with a minister who prayed for her…and in her dream, after he prayed she was healed.

When the woman woke up, she was very confused. From her conversations with John, she knew that we would be in several services after we arrived. He had invited her to come and join us, if she could. But she thought John would be the one preaching. She had never heard of a minister named Richard Roberts, and she didn't know that it was me she was seeing in her dream! It was confusing and just a little frightening to her.

Some people might not have come to the service after that experience. She certainly didn't feel like coming; she told John later that she'd had a horribly severe headache the day of the service.

But this woman wanted to be *healed*…and not just wanted, she *intended* to be healed! Just like the woman in Matthew 9 with the issue of blood, she was willing to do what she had to do to just "touch the hem of Jesus garment" so she could be healed.

Unknown to either John or me, his aunt-in-law came to the service which was to be in a church. It was a huge building and John didn't even know she was there. After the service, we had gone upstairs to the pastor's office to have lunch. John's aunt-in-law had stayed in the church, hoping to get to meet John. Somehow, she had run into my daughter Jordan downstairs and asked her if she could tell her where John had gone. Jordan immediately came upstairs to where we were starting our lunch, and told John that there was someone downstairs who really needed to talk to him. Not knowing for sure who it was, he stepped out of the pastor's office and went downstairs.

When she saw John, the woman rejoiced with him and told him that they had been praying for us, and had been eagerly waiting for the service for more than a week. John was thrilled to finally meet her, and invited her to come up to have lunch with us.

When they approached our table, John introduced me to his aunt-in-law, and he just briefly told me that they had been praying for her for some time because she had HIV/AIDS. He asked me if I would pray with her.

Very quietly and without attracting any undue attention, I laid my hands on this precious woman and prayed. And I knew nothing else until weeks later. That's when John told me what she had told him…that when I prayed, she felt the power of God go through her until she felt weak in the knees.

After lunch at the church, she and John went for dessert somewhere where they could visit with each other more. She told John about her dream of being healed, and how she no longer had the terrible headache she'd had all day before prayer. She believed that God had healed her of HIV/AIDS that very day, and John believed it too.

As we returned home and John and his wife continued to hear from this relative in Kenya, she'd say, "Oh, I'm feeling so well!" They learned that all the boils and lesions on her face had disappeared. She no longer needed her regular medication to help her feel better and she was gaining new strength every day. In fact, almost immediately after the service that day she was able to do all her work by herself, without any help, and was even able to prepare a big meal for her daughter when she came home from school to visit.

After several months, John's aunt-in-law returned to her doctor and had the antibody test retaken that she'd had when she had first been diagnosed with HIV/AIDS. The test results came back negative! The doctor could find no signs of the disease anywhere!

This woman is healed from HIV/AIDS...and it has even been confirmed by her doctor.

Don't Ever Give Up

What I really want you to see about this woman in Africa is that she could easily have given up before her healing ever came. But she didn't! She chose to claim or "pull down" the healing that she believed God wanted to give her and that she saw coming to pass in her dream, even when she didn't know how to interpret that dream.

That day of the service, she could have stayed home. She could have thought, "Well, if God wants to heal me He can come to where I am." She had a severe headache and wasn't feeling strong. She didn't really know John, or if she'd see him in the service, but she made sure she found him after it was over. And she certainly didn't know that it was me she had seen in her dream. But she believed that she would be healed, and she was intent on getting to that service that day.

Then after I prayed for her and she and John were alone, she began speaking out of her own mouth that she believed she was healed. She began doing things at home that she couldn't normally do before. And finally she went and was tested again to be sure to have medical proof of her healing.

In her actions, and the actions of many other people I've observed through the years who have come to my services or contacted our ministry in some other way, I see the fulfillment of Matthew 11:12, where the "violent"—those who have an ardent zeal—seize their miracles by force.

I've heard the expression, "Without God, I cannot...but without me, He will not." And I believe it to be true. God will not do it all for us. He has given us His only Son to die for our sins and purchase our salvation, healing, and deliverance. He has given us His Holy Spirit to live inside of us and guide us into all truth and into His will for our lives. And He has given us His Holy Word with all the instructions we need to live the godly and blessed abundant life He has designed for us.

Now it's up to us. Now we must "take it by force." We must stand strong in the battle against our enemy, Satan, and fortify—or strengthen—our inner man with God's Word so that we don't fall apart every time he comes against us to try and cheat us out of God's blessings.

Picture an army doing battle. What good would the soldiers be if every time they were attacked, or even threatened to be attacked, they fell apart or just dropped their weapons and ran? They wouldn't be much help, would they? That's why they go through long weeks and months of training—learning how to handle their weapons and how to trust their commanding officer—so that when an attack comes, as it inevitably will, they're ready.

Jesus told us in John 16:33 that in this world, we *would* have tribulation—trials, sorrows, and frustrations—but that we could still rejoice and be "of good cheer," because He has already overcome the world through His death and resurrection. He has already defeated every work of the devil (1 John 3:8), including sickness and disease, poverty, sin, emotional illnesses, family problems, broken relationships, addictions, compulsions, and anything else that is not part of His abundant life. And He sees us as healed and whole, physically, mentally, and spiritually. Our job is to begin to see ourselves as God sees us, to *live by our faith*, and not by what we see in the natural, which the Bible tells us to do in four different verses (Habakkuk 2:4, Romans 1:17, Galatians 3:11, Hebrews 10:38).

Put on Your Armor

To walk by faith we need to put on the full armor of God described in Ephesians 6, which includes the **shield of faith**—with which we can quench all the fiery darts of the wicked one (v. 16), the **helmet of salvation**—protecting our minds by taking off the world's way of thinking and putting on the mind of Christ, by letting the Word wash us and transform us by the renewing of our mind (v.17), and the **sword of the Spirit** (v. 17)—the Word of God. God's Word is *alive and full of power—making it active, operative, energizing and effective…sharper than any two-edged sword* (Hebrews 4:12 AMP).

When we know who we are based on God's Word, we can withstand whatever the devil throws our way, and when we're walking by faith and not by sight, we see ourselves as God sees us—in the way that John's aunt-in-law saw herself healed and whole from HIV/AIDS.

I can't encourage you strongly enough to get into God's Word and begin to confess it over your life. Begin to take those precious promises from God and hold onto them as if they were written to you personally…because they were.

As you read and study God's Word, find verses that apply to your particular sickness or problem that you're facing and begin to quote those verses out loud over yourself. Put your own name into the Scripture to make it more personal. For instance, instead of just reading from John 3:16, "God so loved the world that He gave His only begotten Son," begin to declare out loud, "God so loved **Mary** (or Tom, or whatever your name is) that He sent His only begotten Son that **I** should have eternal life."

Instead of reading Isaiah 53:5 as, "by His stripes, we are healed," declare "by Jesus stripes, **I am** healed."

When you're reading a passage of Scripture out loud, read it in first person (using personal pronouns I, me, mine) *and* include your name. Such as when you're reading Proverbs 4:20–22, declare,

I give attention to God's words;

I incline my ear to His sayings.

I do not let them depart from my eyes;
I keep them in the midst of my heart;
For they are life to **me**, who has found them,
And health to all **my** flesh.

Do whatever you need to do to make God's Word alive and real to you. The Word of God is our best defense against the devil. It's what Jesus Himself used when Satan came to tempt Him and try to keep Him from His destiny of dying on the Cross and making salvation and healing possible for you and me.

As God's Word comes alive in you, I believe you will begin to see yourself as God sees you. You'll be able to identify with who you are in Him, rather than identifying with the disease, or overwhelming situation you're facing.

According to God's Word:

You are *not* your illness…

You are *not* your addiction…

You are *not* your financial problem…

You are *not whatever it is* that the devil would like you to become.

When you have accepted Christ as your Savior,

You are a *child of God* (Romans 8:16)…and *Jesus' friend* (John 15:15).

You are the *righteousness of God in Christ* (2 Corinthians 5:21).

You are a joint *heir with Jesus Christ Himself* of all that is in the earth and all that is stored up for you in heaven (Romans 8:17).

You are an *overcomer* (Romans 8:37).

You are the *head and not the tail* (Deuteronomy 28:13).

You are a *citizen of heaven* (Philippians 3:20), seated with Christ in heavenly places (Ephesians 2:6).

You are *God's temple* (1 Corinthians 3:16), *God's co-worker* (1 Corinthians 3:9), and *God's workmanship* (Ephesians 2:10).

You can enjoy the *best of the land* (Genesis 45:18).

You are *healed and whole* (Isaiah 53:5; 1 Peter 2:24).

You have been *bought with a price* (1 Corinthians 6:20), *redeemed and forgiven* (Colossians 1:14), and *set apart for God* (Romans 1:1). You are *forever free from condemnation* (Romans 8:1–2), *established, anointed, and sealed by God* (2 Corinthians 1:21–22).

As a follower of Christ, you are *the salt and light of the earth* (Matthew 5:13–14), you have *constant access to God through the Holy Spirit* (Ephesians 2:18), and you are *His ministers of reconciliation* on this earth (2 Corinthians 5:17–18).

Philippians 4:13 tells us that you and I *can do all things through Christ who strengthens* us, and Romans 8:37 reminds us that *we are more than conquerors through Him that loved us.* In Christ, you and I have all we need to live a victorious life and all we need to live in a godly manner (2 Peter 1:3). I believe that if we want to live in the victory God promises us in His Word, we need to know who we are in Christ, then renew our commitment to believing and being who His Word says we really are.

I tell you, on the authority of God's Word, that our God is *El Shaddai*, the God of *more than enough!* He is not the God of just getting by, or the God of minimums. He is *more than enough!* In His presence, there is more than enough healing for our physical bodies, and more than enough restoration for our relationships, finances, and more. He has more than enough power and supply to meet every need.

Our part is to confess the truth of God's Word, to believe it, and to receive it.

You may want to do as my dad did in the last years of his life and memorize several Scriptures or portions of Scriptures—Dad sometimes memorized a whole chapter—that are personally meaningful to you, so that you can repeat them out loud. Dad used to do that in the morning when he woke up, at night before he went to sleep, and other times when he needed the strength and power of God's Word. Dad said that nothing had ever helped him to stay strong in the Lord into his 90s like memorizing and confessing these Scriptures out loud several times every day.

At the end of this book, I've included a list of Scriptures that you may want to consider using to confess over your life. Many of them are verses or passages that Lindsay and I used when we recorded our healing CD called *He Sent His Word and Healed Them*. Or you may want to pick your own Scriptures that have meant the most to you and can help you believe God for your total healing.

I encourage you to make this a daily practice, and as you agree with God's Word and confess it over your life, I believe it will help you "pull down" God's promises into your life and begin to walk in the miraculous abundance God already has prepared for you.

Chapter 9
OBSTACLES TO HEALING

I've said in this book that sickness and dis-ease—however they are affecting our lives—do not come from God; they are works of the devil. Jesus came to destroy those works, according to 1 John 3:8, so based on that Scripture, and many others, we know that we can call on Him to heal us. And sometimes healing is no more complicated than that. It may not happen overnight; it may take time and prayer, getting God's Word in our hearts and confessing it over our lives, but our healing comes to us in what you could call a "straightforward" kind of way.

But there are also times when there may be **obstacles to our healing**...and some of those obstacles can be things that we have done, whether knowingly or unknowingly, and may require us to make some changes in our lives to experience God's total healing.

That's what I want to talk to you about in this chapter. I feel like I would be remiss if I wrote a book to help you get healed and then failed to touch on some of these more difficult, sometimes even emotional, subjects.

What are some of the obstacles to healing? I'm going to touch on four areas that I believe have probably caused obstacles to more people's healing or restoration to wholeness than any other that I know of. Those four obstacles are:

1. unforgiveness and bitterness
2. taking offense
3. unrepentant sin (a pattern of sin we have not confessed to God and asked His forgiveness for), and
4. the influence of demonic spirits.

This Is Not a "Ticket" to Judge People

Some people may believe that all sickness is a result of something that we have done wrong. And they have used that judgment as a club to beat people with. But I certainly don't believe that way, and neither did Jesus. Jesus put that idea to rest once and for all in John 9. A man who was blind from birth came to Jesus for healing. The disciples asked Jesus this all-important question about the cause of this man's physical problem. They said, *"Rabbi, who sinned, this man or his parents, that he was born blind?" Jesus answered, "Neither this man nor his parents sinned"* (vs. 2–3).

Jesus was telling the disciples that no one had done anything to cause the man's blindness; it was no one's fault that he had been born that way. Then in the next verse, He went on to tell them that because he *was* blind, people could now see the wonderful works of God revealed in him when he was healed.

No matter what has caused the physical illness or other terrible hurt that you are facing, God wants to show forth His glory and heal you. But if you're holding onto something that's causing the pain, there may be something He needs you to do first, so He can bring you relief and healing and others can see His wonderful works in your life.

1. Unforgiveness and Bitterness

One of the most difficult things that I have ever had to do personally is to forgive someone who has hurt me, or hurt someone I love. I think it's probably the most difficult thing that any of us ever have to do. It's something that our human flesh just doesn't want to do.

When someone comes against you to hurt you, or blacken your name, or cause other people to think badly of you, there is that fleshly part of you that wants to strike back, that wants to tell your story, that wants to exonerate yourself—or show yourself to be not guilty of what the other person has accused you of.

Why do we have to forgive people who have hurt us? *Number one, because Jesus told us to.* In Matthew 18:21–22, Peter had been hurt and asked Jesus how many times he had to forgive his brother…was it *seven* times? he asked Jesus.

Now that sounds like a lot of times to me, doesn't it to you? But Jesus told Peter that he must forgive, not just seven times, but **70 times seven.**

Forgiveness is that important to Jesus. In fact, it's so important that He told us in Matthew 6:15 AMP, *if you do not forgive others their trespasses [their reckless and willful sins, leaving them, letting them go, and giving up resentment], neither will your Father forgive you your trespasses.* Who doesn't need God's forgiveness for their sins? So we must forgive one another.

But even beyond that, God did not create us as human beings to carry the awful burden of bitterness and unforgiveness. I believe if you carry those kind of negative emotions in your heart long enough, it will make you physically and emotionally ill.

One of the best examples I can give you is that medical science has drawn connections between some illnesses and holding bitterness or hatred in our hearts. There are times when arthritis, and other kinds of muscle and joint-type diseases, may be caused—or at least made much worse—by someone who is holding on to bitterness. Now that doesn't mean that *all* arthritis or similar illnesses are caused that way. But sometimes they are.

An orthopedic surgeon once told me that before he agrees to do surgery, he will often ask his patients questions about bitterness in their relationships. He says, "If I find that the patient has bitterness towards someone, my surgery has a much better chance of working successfully if I can pray with them first and help them let go of that bitterness before surgery."

That's what I mean when I say that our bodies are not designed to carry the heavy toll of unforgiveness and bitterness. It ends up hurting us, the one carrying the bitterness, rather than the person we're holding the bitterness toward. Lindsay has a good way of explaining this. I've heard her say, "**holding bitterness or unforgiveness in your heart against someone is like drinking poison…and expecting the other person to die.**" It doesn't happen that way, does it? Bitterness and unforgiveness usually end up hurting *us* in the long run.

So what do we do when someone has hurt us, or hurt someone we love very dearly? We give that hurt to God in prayer, and ask God to help us forgive that person. Then comes the really hard part. We must **make the *choice* to forgive**. We must **choose to let go** of that thing that we've been holding onto against that person who has hurt us.

Many people mistakenly believe that forgiveness is a feeling. They think, "I can't forgive until I *feel* forgiveness for that person." But I believe that's completely backwards: **forgiveness is a choice**. You may or may not feel anything. But making the decision to forgive, and letting go of the right that you feel you've had to hold anger and bitterness against them, that's all God is asking you to do. He's not asking you to feel wonderful warm feelings for them, or necessarily to befriend them again. It may not even be wise to befriend someone whose judgment you no longer trust. But God does ask you to make the choice with your will to let go of your judgment against them. And many times when you do that, your feelings will eventually fall in line.

Now, how do you really do this? How do you operate by your spirit when you've been used to operating in the flesh? Sometimes I say to myself, "Down, flesh!" and I literally command my flesh to submit to my spirit. But you have to mean it. You have to **avoid entertaining those thoughts** when Satan tries to bring them back to your mind…and he will try! You must cast them, or throw them, down off the throne where they have become like a "stronghold" in your mind, taking the place of God's Word in your life. And fortunately, God has given us the power to do that. Second Corinthians 10:4–5 tells us,

> *For the weapons of our warfare are not carnal but mighty in God for pulling down strongholds, casting down arguments and every high thing that exalts itself against the knowledge of God, bringing every thought into captivity to the obedience of Christ.*

Many times in my life, I've had to cast down negative, deadly emotions. Many times I've had to cast down negative thoughts about people—people who have maligned me, who have said all kinds of unkind or untrue things, who have had an agenda against me, or my family, or even against our ministry. But no matter what the motivation behind it, we're not called to judge them. We're called to forgive. You have to come to the place where you say, just as Jesus had to say, "Father, forgive them, for they don't know what they're doing" (Luke 23:34).

How hard must that have been for Jesus to say that? These were His own people who turned against Him. One of His own, Judas, was the person who actually betrayed Him. Yet He forgave, He who had done no wrong…who had never known any kind of sin…ever. I believe Jesus is our example. If He could forgive, surely in our imperfection *we* can forgive.

Then there's another step the Bible tells us to take, even beyond just forgiving them. In Matthew 5:44–45, He tells us, *bless those who curse you, do good to those who hate you, and pray for those who spitefully use you and persecute you, that you may be sons of your Father in heaven; for He makes His sun rise on the evil and on the good, and sends rain on the just and on the unjust.*

God doesn't ask us to do that because those who persecute us deserve to be treated that way, but because He wants to develop His character in us and He wants others to see that we are our Father's children.

Well, that's very hard to do, isn't it? When someone is sticking a knife in your back, it's hard to bless them. In fact, it's even hard to know *how* to bless them. What does that Scripture even mean?

I was recently having a conversation with a minister friend about that very subject. I asked him, "How do you bless them?" He said, "Let me tell you how I once blessed another minister who came against me." He said, "I sent him an offering. I didn't do it to try and change him. I did it because I felt the Lord telling me to. But over the months, that man totally changed toward me. First thing I knew, he had invited me to lunch and we had begun to build a new relationship."

Now that doesn't mean that everyone who forgives someone needs to get back into a personal relationship with them. But these men once truly loved each other, and God worked a miracle of restoration in their lives.

There are all kinds of ways to do good, or plant seed, in someone's life. I remember a time when I was in Africa. There was a man who was the leading pastor of the largest ministry in the city where we were, and he was very upset that I was in his town and was coming to preach. For weeks before I came, he preached against me...in spite of the fact that I'd never even met this man.

I learned of his preaching against me when I arrived in his area. Well, I prayed about it, and I felt the Lord telling me something He wanted me to do. When I got to our hotel, I asked someone to get me the minister's phone number, and I called him. When he came on the line, I called him by his name, and I said, "I'm Richard Roberts with the Oral Roberts Ministries. I'm here to preach a healing crusade beginning tonight. I know we've never met, but I've heard some wonderful things about your ministry. I just wanted to call and say 'thank you' for your prayers. I've come with no agenda of my own for your country; just to preach, to win people to Christ, and to pray for the sick and see God do miracles. I don't know what your plans are, but I would love for you to sit on the platform at my services, and that's why I'm calling: to invite you to come."

I hung up not knowing if he would come or not, but I did what I felt God had told me to do. He never did come to my service, but something was changed in his attitude toward me, and over the years we built a relationship. And to this day, I have a standing invitation to his ministry any time I want to go.

I believe that's one of the best ways you can bless someone. Just go directly to the person…and don't counter their meanness with more meanness. Counter it with love. As 1 Thessalonians 5:15 says, "Repay evil with kindness."

I would encourage you not to be confrontational with people, generally speaking. I think many times today, people have become confrontational and angry because they see that kind of behavior in the media every day. But I don't find that in Jesus, and I don't find it in His Word. I see that we are to love our enemies.

One thing that may help when you have been hurt is to remember it's inevitable that it's going to happen…and often it happens within your own circle, just as it did with Jesus. Jesus told us to remember that if He was persecuted, we would be persecuted also (John 15:20). So all of us will come up against times when we have to forgive.

If you're holding onto some hurt that you've experienced, and you rehearse it over and over in your mind, each time clenching your fist (or maybe your emotions) harder and harder, I believe it's important for you to consider that that unforgiveness and bitterness might be an obstacle to your healing.

There's a story of a little boy who got his hand stuck in an expensive vase. His parents and others worked over and over to try and get that vase off of his hand, until finally one person said, "There's only one way. We'll just have to smash that vase and then we can pull his hand out." At the thought of going through that painful experience, the little boy looked up at his parents and sheepishly asked, "Would it help if I let go of the quarter I'm holding?"

Just as the orthopedic surgeon I know encourages his patients to let go of any unforgiveness they're holding so that his surgery has the best chance to work, if you've been nursing a grudge against someone and not allowing God to help you forgive, I encourage you to do it now…so that God's healing power can have the best chance to work in your life and make you whole again.

You may have been carrying those deadly negative emotions in your heart for many years…or it may just have started not long ago. Whatever your situation is, today is your today to get free. When you let go of unforgiveness, I can't promise you that it will change the other person's heart. But I can promise you that it will change you…and that's what really matters in your need for healing.

How do you do it? Where do you begin? Begin by saying, "God, I can no longer carry the hurt of unforgiveness against this person. Right now, I surrender it to You. I can't handle them, and I know You can. So I'm giving this person to you, along with these deadly negative emotions I've been carrying."

I've had to do that many times in my life, and I expect I'll have to do it some more in the future. At times, I hold my hands out in front of me, as if I'm holding something in them, and I say, "God, I give this person to You. By my faith, I choose to forgive _____" …and I say the person's name. Sometimes I say it over and over, so I can hear myself forgiving them.

If there's more than one person you've been holding bitterness for, just list them all. Say, "I forgive John. I forgive Bill. I forgive Mary. I forgive Jim," or whatever their name may be.

And when Satan comes back to remind you about that person—which I can guarantee you he will—just tell him, "Satan, I've forgiven that person." If he comes back a second time, say it again. Just keep saying it until the devil leaves you alone, because James 4:7 says that when we resist the devil, he *will* flee.

If you have thoughts or imaginations of getting even that keep coming to you, just cast them down. It may not happen overnight, but it won't be long until your old thoughts and feelings of revenge will disappear. And you won't have to live with the awful toll of taking vengeance on someone. *Vengeance is mine*, says the Lord, *I will repay* (Romans 12:19). If there's any repaying to be done, God will do it. Only He can absorb the toll. You and I cannot.

2. Taking Offense

Some people wear **offenses** as a badge. You may know someone like that…or perhaps you *are* someone like that. Many times they live life stuck in unhappiness, forcing those around them to live through it with them, because they continually get their feelings hurt by other people. They take everything personally. But we can't go through life taking everything that other people say and do against us personally.

Not picking up offenses is a constant battle that everyone faces. And it's one we have to stay on top of, or it can grow into an unbearable monster. It's easy to assume that when someone hurts your feelings they are aware that they did it, and they did it *intentionally*. That's probably the first thought that tries to plant itself in your mind.

That's just like Satan, isn't it? He takes advantage of every opportunity, and when our feelings are hurt, he goes directly for the kill...making us decide that the other person purposely intended to hurt us, when often that is not the case at all. In fact, there are probably many times when there was no intention whatsoever to hurt us...they didn't even know that they did, because we misunderstood what they meant and took what they said the wrong way. Or what someone *told* us someone else said. Many offenses come to us "secondhand," and we still take great offense. From "well-meaning" friends who don't know better than to repeat something that *they* may have taken out of context in the first place. Or sometimes we pick up the offenses of other people, things that have happened to our friends and loved ones.

In case you're tempted to think that carrying offenses is not very serious business with God, listen to what Jesus said in Matthew 18:7, *Woe to the world because of offenses! For offenses must come, but woe to that man by whom the offense comes!*

God does not want us to live our lives offended. Nor does He want us to carry tales of offense to others, or to be the source of offending someone else. Perhaps more than in any other area, **our pride becomes inextricably intertwined with taking offenses**. And being in a position of pride is not a good place to be when we are praying and asking God for a miracle, for James 4:6 tells us that *God resists the proud but gives grace to the humble.*

Many of our ministry partners know that I get up early every morning before sunrise and seek the Lord in prayer. I think that time alone with Him has kept me strong. It's always a good time to examine my own heart and ask God, as David did, to remove those things from my heart that are not like His heart.

I remember an experience I had one morning during my prayer time with the Lord where He began to show me people that I had hurt or offended in some way through the years. As He showed me, I truly repented of each one, and I asked the Lord to forgive me for what I had done. I thought that was all there was to it. But then He told me that I was to begin to go to these people, in whatever way I could, and offer them my personal apology.

Talk about your pride being involved! Talk about something I didn't want to do! This was definitely it! First of all, I didn't even know if some of these people would remember what I might have done to offend them. And second, I didn't know what their reaction would be if they *did* remember. But after arguing with the Lord and with myself for awhile, I knew that I needed to do what the Lord was telling me to do.

As it turned out, many people reacted in a gracious way to my apologies. Let me give you a specific example of how one man reacted.

Several years ago, this man worked for our ministry. I didn't think he was doing a good job, and I rode him pretty hard. I really didn't want him to stay at our ministry, and over a period of time, I devised a plan in my mind to get rid of him. I did everything I could think of. I undercut this guy. I said things to him that would have offended anyone and caused them to think of leaving, and I just made his life miserable in general.

The interesting thing to me was that when God spoke to me about him, before giving me any instruction related to this man, He said to me, "Richard, in doing what you've been doing, you are setting yourself up for someone else to do the same thing to you." I knew what He was saying because I knew the Scripture in Galatians 6:7 that says, *Do not be deceived, God is not mocked; for whatever a man sows, that he will also reap.* So I knew this was a very serious matter to the Lord. He told me, "I want you to repent, and I want you to make things right with him."

I did what God asked me to do. I repented in my prayer time with Him. Then I went to see the man I had offended. I sat down with him, and I confessed, "I have done you wrong. I've even tried to run you off." And he shook his head as I talked, because he knew it. I said, "God spoke to me and told me that I was wrong to do what I did. I have repented and asked Him to forgive me, and now I'm telling you how wrong I was and asking for your forgiveness. Will you forgive me? I'm so sorry for hurting you."

That man could have reacted in a million different ways. I wasn't sure what would happen. It took all the courage I had to go see him eye-to-eye. But he turned to me and said an interesting thing. He said, "Richard, my respect level for you has just gone back up to where it used to be." And over time, our relationship was healed...and my respect for him rose to new levels, as well.

You see, we try to make excuses about our actions. We try to blame everything on the devil, when sometimes that thing coming against us is not coming from the devil. It's coming from our own wrong or hurtful actions that we brought on ourselves. It's a harvest from the bad seeds we've sown, coming home in a harvest of pain.

Now don't misunderstand me in this. Satan has an agenda against you. He's trying to kill, steal, and destroy those who were created in God's image, which is the human race. He's af-ter everyone. He hates all of us. But in particular, he's definitely after those who are serving God, because when he looks at us it reminds him of what Jesus looks like. And what really makes him mad is when we *talk* like God!

I think the reason it's so easy for Satan to be as cunning and clever as he is is the fact that he was there early on. Originally, he was in heaven with God, so he knew God's plan to create mankind. And he knows every weakness we have. He understands humanness and humanity. Therefore he comes at you in your weakest moment, your most vulnerable point, and that's where he attacks you.

So there's plenty of blame that belongs to the devil. And it was the devil who tempted me in the first place to treat the man badly. But I didn't have to give in to the temptation. I could have resisted him and he would have had to flee. I wanted to do what I did, because I wanted that man to quit.

Country and western star Dolly Parton tells a story about having her hair piled up on top of her head when she was young. Her parents were appalled, and didn't want their daughter dressing and looking like she did. When her mother saw Dolly, she said, "Dolly, the devil must have made you do that." "No, Mama," Dolly said. "I did that all by myself!" And that describes the story I just told you about my own life.

Many times we are our own worst enemy. By our own words and actions, we end up setting ourselves up for failure, when God wants to set us up for miracles, instead.

Think of all the negative confessions you've said about people that you don't like or that may have offended you for one reason or another…or people you have offended. Those words aren't just spoken and then fall to the ground and disintegrate like snowflakes. No. Our words are still hanging out there somewhere. Our words are important. They have "sticking power." So if we've said negative things about people, especially untrue things, we need to cancel them out.

How? First, by repenting. Second, by beginning to say the opposite—positive words of faith and truth. And, third, by going to the person we've wronged and apologizing for it...when it's appropriate to do that. It's important that we listen to the Holy Spirit in that area, because sometimes it may do more harm than good to try and apologize. You must use discernment in that area. In the case of the man I told you about, God specifically told me to go and apologize to him. But that might not be the case in every situation.

There's an old expression that people sometimes teach their children to encourage them not to let everything in life get them down. It says, "Sticks and stones may break my bones, but words can never hurt me." I understand the intent of that. But I also know that the words we say can, and often do, hurt people very badly.

You may not realize what you've done at the moment. But it's a negative seed that you've planted. And if you don't try and cancel those negative seeds out by replanting good seeds in their place, they will come up in a negative harvest that will set you up for failure down the road.

It's not that God doesn't want to intervene and help us. But God is bound to His Word—that is eternal and everlasting. And when we plant negative seeds, we literally tie God's hands behind His back, because He is bound to carry out His Word. He said that whatever we sow, we will reap. He can't change His Word.

Not only *can't* He change His word, but He *won't* change it. Jeremiah 1:12 tells us that He watches over His word to perform it. So unless you do something to change the seed that you sow, every negative seed will come back to you multiplied...just as every positive seed is multiplied, as well.

Unfortunately, one of the biggest areas where Christians take offense is in the area of the churches we go to or the ministries we support. America has been what I call "cafeteria-ized" in our churches. We often pick and choose what we want to agree with and not agree with. It's like walking through a cafeteria line and saying, "I like that item, so I'll take one of those, but I don't like that item, so I'll ignore that." We hear one of our ministers say something we don't agree with, and we begin saying, "Oh, I don't like that guy, or that woman, anymore." We're too sophisticated; we've been cafeteria-ized in this country.

I like to fish. And I've been marlin fishing off the east coast of Florida. The marlins there are very sophisticated. You have to use live bait—and sometimes you even have to use a kite so you don't drown the bait by pulling it behind the boat, because the marlin need to see the live bait swimming or they become wary. They're hard to catch because they have been "fished" a lot and they know what to look out for. That's what I mean when I say they're very sophisticated fish.

But if you go fishing just 150 miles away in the Bahamas, the marlins there aren't nearly as sophisticated. You can take a frozen piece of fish, put it on your line behind the boat, and catch a 200-pound marlin. I know because I've done just that. Those fish are not sophisticated; they're just hungry.

I believe that's often the story of Christianity in America. Many Christians are so "sophisticated" or cafeteria-ized that they get offended when they hear one little thing they don't like, and they throw the baby out with the bathwater. They've not used wisdom in accepting the fact that we're probably never going to accept 100% of anybody's teaching. But we can take the 75 or 80% that we do agree with, realize that our ministers are limited human beings just like everyone else is, and not throw the baby out with the bathwater…and not get so offended.

I believe that's the number one reason behind so much of the church-hopping that goes on. Immature Christians hear something that offends them and they move on to someplace else. They regularly hop from one church or one ministry to another. You've probably heard conversations like this take place:

"Where have you been to church lately?"

"Well, I've been to so-and-so church last year, and then the year before that I went to another church across town. It just seems like every church I go to, something happens that really offends me."

It seems like, to me, that someone like that is just the kind of person who likes to get offended...by everything, everywhere they go. God doesn't want us to be like that. He wants us to grow up and mature, and stop allowing ourselves to be offended by everything we don't like or agree with, or by someone who may have accidentally hurt our feelings. We need to realize that there are going to be times when something offends us or hurts our feelings, just as Jesus said, and when it does we need to forgive that person, remember that they're imperfect just as we are, and that we sometimes hurt other people ourselves.

If you're one of those people who gets offended easily and holds on to hurt feelings with a vengeance, that can be a stumbling block to healing. I believe that as we close up our minds and our hearts to other people, we often close ourselves up to God's influence as well. Maybe you don't get offended by your pastor, but you let your friends and relatives know on a regular basis that they have offended you. And you sulk in your hurt feelings, and make people pay for what they've done.

Every time you do that, I believe you're planting negative seeds. And those negative seeds will one day come back in a terrible harvest that you don't want to reap. In fact, they may have already come back to you in a heart and a spirit that has become tough and hardened, even towards the Lord.

Right now, you can take a positive action to cancel out those negative seeds. You can ask the Lord to forgive you for taking such offense at what other people have said or done to you, or what you may have incorrectly *thought* that they said or did. You can give those offenses to God, and ask Him to help you, as David did. In Psalm 51:10 David prayed, *Create in me a clean heart, O God; and renew a right spirit within me.*

Then begin to replace your negative words with positive words of gratitude, thanksgiving, and praise. I believe you'll find it making a difference in your life and it can open you up more to the possibilities of what God can do in your life.

3. The Sin Issue

Another area that can be a blockage to healing in our lives is in the area of sin. Now I'm not talking so much about the kinds of mistakes and failings that we all make as human beings that we later realize and repent of. In Romans 3:23, we're told that *all have sinned, and come short of the glory of God.* So we must deal with the sin issue in our lives, no matter what kind of sin it is.

Let's look at the man who couldn't walk in Mark 2:1–12 who was lowered through a roof into the presence of Jesus by his four friends. Jesus saw the four friends had faith. But what was the first thing He said to the paralyzed man on the mat? He said, "Your sins are forgiven."

Why did Jesus do that? Apparently He perceived that there was sin in the man's life. And perhaps his lifestyle of sin had had an effect on his very health. So Jesus dealt with the sin issue first. I think that's because when you have unrepentant sin in your life, you know it. No one else may know it. You may have grown very adept at hiding it. But you know it's there. The one person you never fool is yourself.

And when the Holy Spirit comes to convict you of the sin—meaning to lead you to repent of it—you know what He's trying to deal with you about. No one needs to tell us that we are sinners or that we have sin in our lives. We may not want to, or be ready, to face up to it, but we already know it's there. And that's what the Holy Spirit works on to try and draw us toward God and repentance.

I believe that's what happened that day when they lowered the man into the presence of Jesus—he recognized his own shortcomings, faults, and sins. Jesus saw that in him and responded to it by saying, "Son, your sins are forgiven."

The same kind of thing happened with Peter in Luke 5:1–9 when he saw the miracle catch of fish they had caught at Jesus' direction, after fishing all night and catching nothing. Peter fell on his knees in the boat and said to Jesus, "Lord, depart from me. I'm a sinful man." Jesus saw the same thing in Peter, and later told him, "I'll make something out of your life, Peter. I'll make you a fisher of men." And Peter, in essence, gave his heart to Jesus at that moment.

Everyone has sin in their life. We do and we say things and we entertain things in our lives that are sin. Everyone does; I don't care who you are. That's why we have to pray daily and cast those things off of our lives. That's why we have to repent.

I personally can't remember a day that I haven't repented over something. Sometimes people don't want to say that or admit it because they think they'll lose something in the eyes of other people. But I think it's more honest to admit it. All of us have to deal with the sin issue in our lives.

But what I want to focus on is the kind of sin that we've held on to in our lives, that we've grown accustomed to and even comfortable with, and sometimes allowed to grow and fester like a cancer. I'm talking especially about unrepentant sin—sin that we've not confessed to God, and we continue to resist the Holy Spirit's attempts to convict us of the fact that we're disobeying God and therefore cheating ourselves out of His blessings.

When Sin Becomes More Important
than God's Blessing

Several years ago, a couple came to me for prayer—the woman came first and I led her in a sinner's prayer to accept Christ. Later she called me again and wanted the man that she was living with to come with her for prayer. She told me that he had been involved in some kind of "cult" movement, and they were now living together. They weren't married; they were just living in the same house together.

When she came to me the second time, with her boyfriend, I spent about an hour talking with them, then I led the man in a prayer to receive Christ as well. When we were through praying, the woman asked, "What should we do now?" I said, "Well, you're living outside of what God tells us to do in the Bible; you're not husband and wife, yet you're living together as if you are." And I very honestly told her, "I don't believe God can bless you in an unholy, disobedient union...especially now that you know the difference."

She looked at me with a bit of surprise in her face, and she asked, "What can we do about it?"

I told them, "You need to do one of two things: you either need to get married, if you truly love each other and will commit to making your marriage work—and I'll gladly perform the wedding—or you need to start living apart. You can say, 'God, we recognize now that living together outside of marriage is not Your standard for our lives. We didn't know any better before, but now we do,' and I can lead you in a prayer of repentance. But you cannot go on living together and having sex outside of marriage and expect God to bless your union. It's simply contrary to His Word."

They looked at each other and said, "Yes, you're right. We want to get married. And we may very well ask you to perform the ceremony, Richard."

I said, "Ok. If that's what you're going to do, you need to make the decision right now that until you're married you'll quit living together and you won't have sex anymore...and one of you needs to move out right away so there'll be no temptation to stay together like you are now."

It was very sound biblical advice, and when they said, "Okay, we'll do that," I thought they were serious. But when I heard from them a little later, I learned that they had changed their minds. They were going to go on living together, outside of marriage, and as far as I know they're still living like that today, in that same sinful state.

I see many people who are living exactly the way that young couple was living. They know better...they know they're living wrong according to God's Word, and they're miserable in what they're doing. **But sin has become more important to them than God's blessing**. Their sin is like an old shoe to them—it's become comfortable; they don't want to let go of it. An old pair of shoes is always more comfortable than a new pair, and if you're going to walk in them, you'd choose an old pair over a new pair any day.

God has given us the freedom to choose. We're even free to choose sin over Him. Sometimes that's what we've done in our lives, and in doing that we have inadvertently opened the hedge of protection that would otherwise be around our lives. By our choice, we have opened the door for Satan to move into some area of our lives...and once we finally realize that, we need to repent and close up that hedge so that we can once again walk in God's full blessing.

He Has Promised His Forgiveness When We Ask

Now, I don't want you to get the wrong idea about how God expects us to deal with sin. I don't believe that God is overly sin-conscious, and He doesn't require that of us either. He loves us more than He disapproves of our sin. I don't believe that He wants us to "over-scrub" or to spend all our time trying to find some hidden sin in our lives. Imagine washing your face five or six times a day to try and get clean. Your skin would soon be raw and dry, like sandpaper. And no matter how many times you wash your face, it doesn't make you clean on the inside.

We also need to remember that temptation is not sin. If temptation was sin, then Jesus was a sinner. Hebrews 4:15 tells us that Jesus was *in all points tempted as we are, yet without sin.* He suffered temptation the same way we do. It is not a sin to be tempted. Sin comes in when we make room for and yield to the temptation.

Yes, God has told us that He wants us to confess our sins to Him. And often in the Bible, He would say to someone who had obviously been sinning, *Go, and sin no more.* He doesn't condone our sin for a moment. But He has made us a wonderful promise in 1 John 1:9 that any time we confess our sins, *He is faithful and just to forgive us our sins and to cleanse us from all unrighteousness.*

God is standing ready to forgive us right now and restore us to a relationship of full blessing with Him. If there is unrepentant sin in your life, or if your whole lifestyle is contrary to the Word of God, remember that it can be an obstacle to receiving your healing or some other blessing the Lord may want to give you.

Sin stunts our relationship with God. When we're tempted to sin, we need to ask ourselves, *How is this thing that I'm being tempted to do going to affect what God has for my life?* The gifts or the calling He's given me? Is it going to stunt it? Is it going to cancel it? Am I going to have to go back to "square one" and start all over again, as the children of Israel did who roamed 40 years in the desert because of their sin and disobedience to God—with many of them never seeing the land of milk and honey that God had promised to them?

We're told in Numbers 32:23, *be sure your sin will find you out.* I don't want to put myself in that kind of position…do you? If you don't, I encourage you to examine your heart. As I said earlier, I believe you already know if there is unrepentant sin in your life. If there is, pray this simple prayer with me, from your heart, right now, and let's get what's wrong in your life right with God so that you can feel confident to go boldly before His throne to ask Him for what you need to be made whole.

Heavenly Father, I come before You with sin in my heart. I've been sinning, Lord, and right now I make the decision to stop it. I renounce what I have done and I make the decision to turn that area of my life over to You. I make You Lord of that area of my life. Thank You for Your promise of forgiveness when I repent. I do repent, and I receive Your forgiveness now. Today, by my will, I make the decision, just like You asked the man in the Bible to do, to go and sin no more. Thank You for cleansing me and setting me free, in Jesus' name. Amen.

4. The Influence of Demonic Spirits

I'm not going to say a lot here about the subject of demonic spirits. It seems like some ministers are always looking for a demon spirit under every rock or around every corner. Personally, I don't see that being the case. To say that **every** sickness is caused by a demonic spirit is a statement of ignorance, and sometimes even manipulation, as far as I'm concerned.

But to say that **no** illness is caused by demonic spirits, or that it's not possible that some other unusually grave situation in someone's life could ever be caused by a demon spirit, is just as ignorant. I know that they can. Scripture indicates it in several instances, and I have seen the evidence of it myself, particularly in some foreign nations where demon spirits are tolerated and even worshipped openly.

I'm going to say something here for which I have no absolute medical proof. But based on growing up in my dad's healing and deliverance ministry, and from my own experience of praying for the sick now for more than 30 years, I believe there are different "levels" of sickness. I believe there is a type of sickness that is in this world simply because of the fall of man in the Garden of Eden. But I believe there is another level of sickness, or a "spirit of infirmity" that is satanic.

All sickness comes to take people out...to kill them, which is satanic at its root, because that's Satan's whole purpose in this world—to kill, steal, and destroy, according to John 10:10. But there seems to be a "different level" to some kinds of illnesses— whether physical, or emotional, or in whatever area of our lives. And that kind of illness takes a greater "pressing in" to God for healing to come about.

In any sickness there are at least five very important things that you need to do for your healing, as I've already covered: (1) you need to focus in on God and use every ounce of your faith to believe you can be healed; (2) you need to get other people to go into agreement with you (that's the main reason we pray with people through this ministry 24 hours a day. It's why we send out our anointing oil and our prayer cloths, as I talked about in an earlier chapter); (3) you need to allow your words to be positive words of confession and of healing; (4) you need to seek God and study His Word, meditating on Scriptures, especially healing Scriptures; and (5) you need to get under a church or ministry that has a strong healing anointing and let them hook up their faith with yours.

Then, in some cases, I would add a sixth thing you may need

to do: If you have tried everything you know to do, including the five steps above, and nothing has given you any relief whatsoever, you may need to seek *spiritual deliverance* from a man or woman of God who can operate in the deliverance ministry.

Now I'm not saying this to *most* people in *most* situations—in fact, I would say it's not necessary in 99% of the cases I've known. But that doesn't negate the reality of the cases that do need it. And if you have a particularly difficult or severe type of illness or other condition...it may be an addiction, or some kind of perverse sexual issue, or maybe an abuse issue, or something of that nature...and, especially, if you have opened your life up to demonic influence at some time in the past or present...you may very well need prayer for deliverance.

Not every person that was brought to Jesus had a demon spirit that was causing their infirmity. But there are several cases listed in the New Testament, where Jesus identified the cause of people's affliction as an evil spirit and commanded those evil spirits to come out...such as:

- the man who couldn't speak until a demon was cast out (Matthew 9:32–34).
- the woman twisted and bent over for 18 years, who had a "spirit of infirmity" (Luke 13:10–13).
- the young man known as "Legion" living among the tombs, who had a supernatural kind of strength and cut himself with rocks, who had been a terror to people, but who began to preach the Gospel after he was set free (Mark 5:1–20).

Many people do not believe that demon spirits are just as real today as they were in Jesus' time, that they can live inside of people who have opened themselves up to them, and that they can be commanded to come out of those people by the authority of Jesus' name...but I have seen it, personally. I have been involved in the deliverance ministry. And I have prayed for people to be delivered in some of my services, both here in America and in other countries, as well.

Let me give you a couple of real-life examples of deliverance.

I prayed for a young man some years ago who had a demonic spirit in him. I didn't perceive it at first, just talking to him, until I laid my hands on him to pray. And when I touched him, God showed me the spirit that was inside of him. I discerned the spirit, spoke to it, and commanded that spirit to come out of him. And the young man—actually it was the demon inside of him—let out a blood-curdling scream you could have heard two blocks away.

I saw a fire-like demonic power come out of him. I don't know how to describe it any better than to say that it looked red and white, like fire, and it came out of him when I commanded it to do so. The young man was delivered…and he knew it. He began to weep and cry, because he knew it was gone and he was free of that spirit. It was a spirit of lust, and I saw it come out.

You know, people don't realize what they're doing, nowadays in particular, when they're visiting pornography websites or allowing themselves to get involved with all kind of sexual sin. We've made it cool to be sexually "free" in the world we live in. "Do what feels good" has become many people's agenda. After all, it's not hurting anyone and it's nobody's business but your own. Pornography is often called the "victimless" crime.

But many of those people have not seen what I've seen when a spirit of lust inhabits a person's life…the perversion they will sink to, and the depths of degradation they will allow themselves to experience and cause other people to experience. Spirits of lust are very strong spirits, and they don't want to let go of the person they're inhabiting. They're nothing to fool around with, and if you have opened your life up to that influence, I would encourage you to seek prayer and/or deliverance as soon as you possibly can.

If Satan is telling you it's too late, or that there's nothing that can be done for you now, I assure you that is not true. There is nothing you have done and nowhere you have gone that God cannot reach you with His love and His saving, healing, delivering power. Nothing is too great for God; He can set you free in a moment's time. But just as in any other choice in our lives, it's up to us to stay free.

Another experience happened in one of my services some years ago in Oakland, California. I was on the platform well into my message when suddenly a big guy who was foaming at the mouth came walking down the aisle, cracking a whip over the people's heads and disrupting the service. God gave me discernment that the man had a demon spirit in him. So I commanded him to stop where he was, and for the spirit to come out of him. At that moment the man just wilted and fell to the floor. He dropped his whip and the foam on his mouth melted away.

Most people were shocked; they'd never seen anything like that before. The Lord spoke to me to give an altar call and give people a chance to accept Jesus right then. I was in the middle of my sermon, so for a minute I kind of argued with God because I didn't think it was time. But the Lord persisted and I obeyed Him. There were more than 4,000 people in the building that day, and when I gave the invitation, at least 1,000 of them responded by coming forward for salvation or to rededicate their lives to Jesus. They had seen such a powerful demonstration of God that my message just wasn't necessary anymore. I never even finished it!

You see, one thing I want you to be assured of is that although the devil does have power, his power is limited. His power is never greater than God's, and God has given that same power to us as believers. In fact, Jesus told the disciples in Mark 16:17–18 that casting out demons in His name would be one of the signs that unbelievers would see among those who followed Him (along with healing the sick, and other supernatural events). And I've never seen it fail, that when I have cast a demon or evil spirit out of someone in one of my services, people cannot wait to accept Christ when I give the altar call.

So there is no reason for you to be frightened or hopeless if you think you may need to have someone who is experienced in the deliverance ministry pray that kind of prayer over you or someone you love. I am not afraid to face the devil head on because I know that God has given me authority over him and all of his demons. In fact, when I see what Satan tries to do to God's beloved creation, human beings, it makes me angry.

He has no true authority over us. But he comes against us through fear, intimidation, and through the lustful desires of our own flesh. He can only come into a human being when we give him permission…when we continually rebel against God and open our minds and hearts to things that are based in evil, such as pornography and practices of the occult, and other things that God has told us to stay away from.

For those who do not understand what demons are or where they came from, let me give you just a brief explanation here. The devil was a great angel in heaven, known as Lucifer. For some reason, he chose to rebel against God and even attempted to become like God (see Isaiah 14:12–14). And in his rebellion he—and one-third of the other angels who rebelled with him— were cast out of heaven to roam the dry places of this world for a limited period of time…only until Jesus returns to this earth one day. They are spirits, having no body; but they seek embodiment in a human being to accomplish their evil plans through men, women, or young people who will open the door and let them in.

Once that has happened, they have "possessed" that person and can control certain aspects of their thinking and behavior, depending on what kind of spirit is indwelling the person. Remember I mentioned earlier that I had seen a spirit of lust come out of a man in one of my services.

But there are other kinds of evil spirits. Jesus referred specifically to spirits who, among other things, had caused: a man to be blind and unable to speak (Matthew 12:22), and a woman to be twisted and bent over in her body, from a "spirit of infirmity" (Luke 13:10–13). As I've said before, most illnesses are not specifically caused by evil spirits, but according to Jesus there are some that are.

I do not know all the specifics about demons. But God always gives me the information I need when I am dealing with one in a situation of ministry. And we do know that there are no new demons. The demons that exist are those who fell with Satan from heaven, as I mentioned before.

Demons cannot resist the authority of Jesus' name. Once, when the disciples had been out ministering and returned to where Jesus was waiting for them, they said to Him in amazement,

> "Lord, even the demons obey us when we use your name!" "Yes," he told them, "I saw Satan fall from heaven like lightning! Look, I have given you authority over all the power of the *enemy, and you can walk among snakes and scorpions* [enemies] *and crush them. Nothing will injure you. But don't rejoice because evil spirits obey you; rejoice because your names are registered in heaven*" (Luke 10:17–20 NLT).

I believe Jesus was reminding us that we are not to make Lucifer, referred to after his fall from heaven as Satan, or the devil, more important than he is. But, according to Jesus, it is a fact of life that there are times when his evil spirits must be cast out of people. And when that is necessary, He has given us the power to do just that.

Some people may believe that a born-again Christian can be "possessed" by a spirit. However, I and many other believers do not believe that to be the case. When a person has accepted Jesus Christ as his or her Savior, the Holy Spirit of God comes in to their spirit at that instant, as I taught you earlier, and takes up residence inside of that person. Therefore, I do not believe an evil spirit can be inside of someone when the Holy Spirit is already there. But even so, we always have a choice of who we want to listen to, or what we want to allow ourselves to become involved in.

Unlike Satan, the Holy Spirit is a gentleman. He never forces us to do anything. If a believer wants to disobey God and allow their mind, or their body, to be joined to something that God has told us to stay away from, I believe we are free to do that. But there is a huge price to be paid for disobedience.

Although evil spirits cannot "possess" your spirit as a Christian, they *can* "oppress" you. They can exert a great deal of force and control over your mind and your body when you continue to give them the opportunity, and you may find yourself unable to extricate yourself from their influence without also having prayer to command them to let go of that influence over your life. I believe that many times that is what has happened, especially today when the opportunity to get involved in habitual sin is so easy...as it is in becoming involved in websites that sponsor habitual behavior such as pornography and other types of things.

Pay Attention to God's Warning System

I don't want to spend any more time in this area. I only want to encourage you to consider the need for deliverance prayer if you, or someone you love, has possibly opened up to demonic control, and has exhausted other possible avenues of help.

I believe that God has given us a built-in warning system, particularly for believers, that we need to pay attention to so that we don't get involved in any areas of Satan's domain. You may walk into a room, shake hands with someone, or look at someone and feel that something is wrong. Or you may come upon a website or a movie on TV that gives you a similar feeling. You may not know exactly what it is, but you just know that something doesn't feel right with that person or that thing. I believe that is the Holy Spirit working through us to give us discernment, or the rightful judgment, to stay away. It's God's supernatural warning system to protect us from the enemy, and we would always be wise to heed the Holy Spirit's leading.

But there may have been times when our curiosity and the desires of our own flesh have gotten the better of us, and we didn't heed the warning to stay away. We allowed ourselves to look, and to feel, and to experience. If you have dabbled in areas that God's Word and His built-in warning system have lovingly advised you to stay away from, I encourage you to pray this prayer now and renounce any past, present, or future involvement with Satan's evil devices.

Father, please forgive me for rebelling against You and the warnings You have placed in Your Word and in my own heart. I renounce all involvement I have had with any area controlled by Satan and the forces of darkness—especially my involvement with _____ (mention by name any specific area you have dabbled in, such as pornography, gambling, occult practices, or anything else that is unlike God).

I turn away from the devil and what is wrong and I turn toward You and what is peaceful and right. I ask You to help me keep my focus on the right things. And by a decision of my will I determine that from this day forward I will follow Your Word to me in Philippians 4:8 that says, **whatsoever things are true, whatsoever things are honest, whatsoever things are just, whatsoever things are pure, whatsoever things are** *lovely, whatsoever things are of good report; if there be any virtue, and if there be any praise, think on these things.*

Now we're ready to move on to the last subject I want to talk to you about in this book: looking to the Lord of the Harvest for your healing.

Chapter 10

LOOK TO THE LORD OF THE HARVEST FOR YOUR HEALING

When I was thinking of what to say to you as I close out this book on healing, I felt the Lord telling me to remind you of the importance of looking to Him as the Lord of the Harvest for your healing. In fact, I believe in many cases, **the harvest you're seeking—your healing—may very well come through your seed**. But if you're not expecting it...if you're focusing on the problem and not looking to the Lord of the Harvest...you may not recognize it when it comes.

Let me tell you a story of something I learned from my mother. When I was very young, my mother and I planted a vegetable garden behind our house. At the time, I had no idea what we were really doing. Mother showed me how to put seeds in the ground and cover them over with dirt. Then she explained to me that, right then, we were planting tomatoes. She reached into her apron pocket and she showed me the package the seeds came in. It had a picture of tomatoes on it. I asked her if that was what the tomatoes would look like and she said yes. Then she read me the words written at the very bottom of the seed package. They said, "Guaranteed to grow."

Well, the next day, I went outside expecting to see tomatoes in the garden where we had planted them, just like the ones my mother had showed me. But instead, I saw nothing there but dirt. For several days, I would go out to the garden to check on our tomatoes. I saw tender shoots come up through the ground, but still no tomatoes. After a while I gave up. I didn't see my harvest right away, so I stopped expecting my harvest to come. Then...I put the idea of harvest completely out of my mind. *Maybe it's not ever going to happen*, I thought.

Maybe that's how you feel right now...or how you have felt at times in the past. Maybe you wonder if your healing is *ever* going to come. Listen to what God tells us in Galatians 6:9. He says,

> *"Let us not lose heart and grow weary and faint in ... doing right, for in due time and at the appointed season we shall reap, if we do not loosen and relax our courage and faint"* (Amplified version).

I'd forgotten all about what my mother had read to me from the bottom of the tomato seed package when we planted our seeds that day. She'd pointed to the words and said, "Richard, this says '**Guaranteed to grow.**'"

The seeds came with a guarantee, or a promise, that they would grow...if we planted them according to the package directions and took care of them the way we were supposed to until they'd had time enough to burst up through the ground and grow into a bountiful harvest.

As a boy, I had to learn to expect that the seeds I planted were going to turn into a bumper crop...no matter how long it took...no matter how long all I could see was dirt. Eventually, I was going to get tomatoes. It said so on the package!

And that's exactly what happened. After weeks had passed, my mother said, "It's harvest time. The tomatoes are in." I hadn't been in the garden for a while. But when we got out there, to my amazement the garden looked just like the picture Mother had shown me. It was full of rich, green vines and plump, bright-red tomatoes. In fact, there was an abundance…so many I couldn't count them all.

There's a very important principle here that I don't want you to miss, because it's central to your ability to receive the healing harvest God wants to send you.

If I had been in charge of my harvest, I never would have received one. Why? Because I had given up on the tomatoes. They would have grown, ripened, rotted, and then gone to seed without my ever knowing what it was like to eat one of those juicy, delicious tomatoes. I had simply quit expecting to see a harvest, so I had stopped checking to see if one was there. *I had planted my seed, focused entirely on the seed, and never shifted my focus to the harvest that was **guaranteed** to come.*

God also guarantees a harvest from the spiritual seeds that we plant. Those seeds are also "guaranteed to grow," according to Galatians 6:9, if we don't give up…if we continue to be faithful in our seed-planting in the meantime and in doing what we need to do to encourage those seeds to grow.

What encourages seeds to grow? They have to have **consistent amounts of water**, don't they? In the same way, I believe we need to encourage our healing seeds to grow by watering our mind with the Word of God…that our thoughts and actions might be sanctified and cleansed *with the washing of water by the word*, according to Ephesians 5:26.

The positive seeds you have planted toward your healing—sometimes financial seeds of your faith, along with the seeds of praying for one another, prayer and trusting God for yourself—need daily watering with the Word of God. Keeping God's Word fresh and alive in your heart will help to keep your faith and expectation alive, as well, as *faith comes by hearing and hearing by the Word* (Romans 10:17).

- When you're tempted to give up on your harvest of *physical healing*, water your seeds with positive confessions of faith from verses like: 1 Peter 2:24, "***By Your stripes I am healed,***" and Exodus 15:26, "***You are the God who heals me.***"

- When you're tempted to give up on your harvest of **emotional healing**, water your seeds with positive confessions of faith from verses like: Psalm 147:3, "***You heal the brokenhearted and bind up my wounds***", and 2 Timothy 1:7, "***You have not given me the spirit of fear, but of power, love, and a sound mind.***"

- When you're tempted to give up on your harvest of **financial healing**, water your seeds with positive confessions of faith from verses like: Malachi 3:10, "***Because I've brought my seed to Your storehouse, You are opening up the windows of heaven to me and pouring Me out a blessing I don't have room enough to contain***", and Philippians 4:19, "***You supply ALL my need according to Your riches in heaven by Christ Jesus.***"

- When you're tempted to give up on your harvest of **family relationship healing**, water your seeds with positive confessions of faith from verses like: Jeremiah 29:11, "***Lord, You have plans for a good future for my loved ones and me***", and Proverbs 22:6, "***My children will not depart from the godly way they were trained when they were young.***"

- Or when you're tempted to give up on ANY harvest that you believe God has promised you, no matter what area of your life, water your seeds with positive confessions of faith from verses like: Mark 9:23, "***Lord, all things are possible to me because I believe You***", and 2 Chronicles 16:9, "***You show Yourself strong in my behalf because my heart is right with You.***"

Jesus told us in Matthew 9:37–38, "*The harvest truly is plentiful, but the laborers are few. Therefore pray the Lord of the harvest to send out laborers into His harvest.*"

Notice that God calls Himself the Lord of the Harvest in those verses. What did He mean by what He said? He meant that there aren't many who will sow, or plant seed, and then get into *expectation* that what they sow will come back to them in the form of a "bumper crop" in their lives.

You know, we're living in a difficult time in our economy. There's unrest in the world on almost every hand. It's a time when many people say, "Things are too uncertain to sow to the Lord right now." They want to hold on to their sowing because they can't get a glimpse of the harvest.

But that's exactly the wrong time to stop sowing, or to give up hope on the seeds they have already sown...because it's the time when we may need our biggest harvest ever. And the only way to get it is through looking to the Lord of the Harvest—the God who is more than enough.

Right now, when you're going through a very difficult time in your personal life, you may be tempted at times to stop sowing seeds to the Lord. If so, let me ask you this question: Isn't *now* the time when you need a harvest in your life? And don't you need a *continual* harvest of miracles from the Lord, not just one harvest once in a while?

In order to receive a continual harvest, we need to be continually planting and cultivating our seed. If a farmer only sowed seed one time and gave up if they didn't grow...or if he didn't cultivate the seeds he had already sown and just let them rot in the field or wither away, there wouldn't be any harvest at all would there?

But successful farmers know the importance of consistency in their planting, and their cultivating, in order to reap. And they *expect* to reap. Just as soon as they plant their seeds, they begin consistently *cultivating* them and *expecting* them to grow...and they know just about when they'll be ready to gather in, too.

They don't just stand in the field, gazing at their seed and exclaiming, "What beautiful seed I've planted." No. Once they've planted those seeds, they immediately begin looking to the future. As they do everything they can do to cultivate the seeds, they ready their workers and their equipment for the coming harvest. And as uncertain as "mother nature" can sometimes be, they still plan for a harvest as soon as the seeds are in the ground. In other words, from the beginning they plan for success. Somehow, they successfully begin looking to the future once their planting work is done.

We need to be that same way with the seed we plant unto the Lord. As soon as we have planted our seed—whatever area that seed might be in: such as praying for others, giving finances, spending time in the Word, speaking positive words of confession—we need to look to the Lord of the Harvest for our healing harvest to come in.

God is true...His Word is sure...and what He says He will do. Unlike the weather and other elements that farmers have to contend with once they've planted their seed, there is nothing uncertain about God. With Him, there is not even a *shadow of turning*, according to James 1:17. We can count on God. With Him, our seeds are "guaranteed to grow."

He said in Malachi 3:10 that when you sow, He would *open for you the windows of heaven and pour out for you such blessing that there will not be room enough to receive it.* But He doesn't even stop there. In verse 11 He adds, *And I will rebuke the devourer for your sakes.*

Who doesn't need the devourer, or the devil, rebuked from their life? In some places the economy is eating people up. With heavy unemployment, many institutions and businesses have declared bankruptcy or just closed down altogether. Wouldn't it be wonderful to know that when you plant seed to God, the Lord of the Harvest is going to bless you so much you can't even contain it, and then He's going to push the devil away from your life and tell him, "Stop it! That's enough! You leave my child alone."

That's exactly what happened to a woman—a partner of our ministry—who contacted me not long ago. She had been facing a terrible time financially. She was about to lose her home…and as anyone knows who has had serious financial problems to deal with, nothing can make you much sicker than severe financial problems and worries.

The woman called to give us a wonderful testimony, and tell us what the Lord of the Harvest had done in her life. She had a $136,000 mortgage on her home. Somehow, she had managed to fend off the foreclosure that was constantly looming around the corner. There just wasn't enough money to pay all the bills, and she was struggling every day to keep her head above water. The enemy, Satan, was trying to destroy her life.

Yet she said that for several months she had been planting a consistent monthly seed of $100 into our ministry, in obedience to what she believed God was telling her to do. In spite of the problems she was facing, she believed the answer was to continue to be faithful to God in her giving…not to hold back and give up just because things looked so bad in the natural.

Then one day, she got a phone call that changed her life. Out of the blue, the lending institution that she had her mortgage with called and canceled $100,000 of the $136,000 she owed them.

She said, "Richard, I had been expecting a miracle and I got one!"

I said, "Ma'am, do you realize how much money you would have had to earn in order to pay off a hundred thousand dollars? Why, you'd have had to earn $150,000 to $200,000 to have had enough to pay taxes on and still have enough left over to pay off $100,000 on a mortgage." I said, "You didn't just receive a $100,000 blessing…you received something between $150,000 to $200,000 blessing!" That made her even happier, and we rejoiced together.

Then she said, "Richard, all I have left to pay is $36,000. And I want you to know that I'm sowing another $100 seed to the Lord through your ministry, because I'm in expectation of another miracle!" Already, she was looking to the future and the next miracle God would bring her.

That's when I knew she really **got** it. She truly understood the Bible principles of seedtime and harvest...and about the need to continually plant and cultivate seeds if you want to have a continual harvest.

It's Time to "Switch Gears"
from the Problem to the Answer

I began this book by asking you to picture yourself in a room, alone with your problem, when Jesus came into the room and with His great compassion reached out to heal you. But to some degree, at that point we were still focusing on the problem.

In ending this book, I want to ask you to picture yourself doing something else...and this time, we're going to focus in on the answer.

Picture yourself driving a car with a manual shift. Imagine that manual shift is right there on the floor of the car near you.

When I was a boy in the 1950s, I learned to drive in my grandfather's old 1954 Pontiac. But back then the gear shift was on the column of the steering wheel. We called it "three on the tree"...there was first, second, and third gear, and to drive you had to learn how to put the car into all three gears. You had to learn how to "shift gears" to accelerate and go faster.

Now picture yourself driving that manual shift car, and starting to get on the interstate. For a little while, maybe while you're still on the entrance ramp, you're doing just fine driving about 25 or 30 miles an hour in second gear. But once you get on the highway, other cars begin whizzing by you. The speed limit is 65 miles an hour, and much of the traffic is moving at 70 miles an hour.

People begin honking at you and giving you "special" signals, as if they're wondering what's going on. Why are you driving 30 miles an hour in a 65-mile-an-hour zone? And if you continue driving that slow, the police will probably pull you over at some point, or other drivers will try and honk you out of the way. You're becoming a hazard going at that speed.

What do you do when you need to go faster? You *shift gears.* You can't do 65 miles an hour in low gear, you've got to get it up to a higher gear...so you shift gears into third gear, or fourth gear, and in some cars even fifth gear.

And just like shifting to a higher gear in a car, sometimes we have to make a shift in life. That's what I'm talking about doing once we have planted our seeds and are doing all we can do to cultivate those seeds and bring them to fruition. But remember, only God can bring the harvest. And He has promised us that our seeds will grow. So we must *look to Him*—the Lord of the Harvest—and begin to *expect from Him* the miracles we need, just like the woman did who found a healing for her financial illness when she trusted God to bring it from the seeds she had planted.

Things in your life may not look very good right now. You may wonder how in the world you're ever going to make it. You and I are not in charge of everything that's going on around us. But we are in charge of the seeds that we sow and cultivate. Genesis 26:1–13 tells us that Isaac sowed during a time of famine, or recession, and it wasn't the first famine either. He wanted to leave the area where he was...he wanted to run away. But he listened to God telling him to stay there. And as he obeyed God and sowed his seed in spite of the financial crisis...in spite of what it looked like all around him...Scripture reports that Isaac *reaped in the same year a hundredfold; and the Lord blessed him. The man began to prosper, and continued prospering until he became very prosperous* (vvs 12–13).

Isn't that what you want? To prosper in your life…to increase and do better and better in every area…where there is true miraculous prosperity from the Lord and any illness or disease cannot stand, as it is overtaken by God's blessing. I know that's what I want for my life. And it's what God wants for us, according to 3 John 2:1 KJV. Listen to His Word to you in that verse, where He calls you His *beloved*:

Beloved, I wish above all things that thou mayest prosper and be in health, even as thy soul prospereth.

As you now shift gears to focus on Jesus—the Lord of the Harvest—picture yourself healed and whole and overcome by His blessings. When you've done all that you can do, we're told in Ephesians 6:13 to "stand." We're to draw a line in the sand…say to the devil, "no more"…and take our stand, until we see God's healing and restoring power manifest in our lives.

I'll Stand with You for Miracles

I want to stand *with you* for miracles, especially for the healing miracle you must have. I know what it's like to need a miracle… and to need someone to stand with me in faith until it comes.

I want to be your faith partner…your partner for miracles. Right now, I want to join my faith with yours for healing in every area of life where you have been struggling, and wondering how you're going to make it. And I want you to know that even after I pray with you now, I will continue praying for you as you let me know about other prayer requests you may have. I'll *stand **with you***. We'll draw a line in the sand ***together***…and we won't come out of our faith agreement until your miracle comes.

Let's pray:

*Lord, I thank You for helping us see clearly that You are a **healing***

Jesus. Thank You for Your logos Word to us in the Bible, and for the rhema word You speak to our hearts in such a personal way today. We are listening to You. We hear Your voice when You speak, and we do what You tell us to do.

Thank You for the gift of Your Holy Spirit. We are sensitive to Him and His divine leading in our lives. We ask You to search our hearts and reveal anything to us that we need to do or to change in our lives. We continually plant our seeds and water them with the washing of Your Word, and our obedience to that Word.

And now, Father, when we've done all…we stand. We draw a line in the sand and expect our miracle to come. We shift gears to look to You, the Lord of the Harvest, and we begin making plans for success…for healing…for deliverance…for miracles in every area of our lives.

*Lord, thank You for being the One who told the children of Israel more than 5,000 years ago…and who still tells us today…**I AM** the God who **heals you**.*

Now I set my faith with yours for your healing…your miracle! And I agree with you for it to come forth in your life. And I am expecting it soon, in Jesus' mighty name. Amen and amen.

HEALING SCRIPTURES FOR YOU

Originally compiled for *He Sent His Word and Healed Them* CD by Richard and Lindsay Roberts. Unless otherwise noted, Scriptures are taken from the New King James Version of the Bible.

Healing and Wholeness for Physical Sickness and Disease

1. **EXODUS 15:26** I am the Lord who heals you.

2. **EXODUS 23:25** So you shall serve the Lord your God, and He will bless your bread and your water. And I will take sickness away from the midst of you.

3. **PSALM 23:4** Yea, though I walk through the valley of the shadow of death, I will fear no evil; for You are with me; Your rod and Your staff, they comfort me.

4. **PSALM 30:2** O Lord my God, I cried out to You, and You healed me.

5. **PSALM 103:2,3,5** Bless the Lord, O my soul, and forget not all His benefits: who forgives all your iniq-

uities, who heals all your diseases, who satisfies your mouth with good things, so that your youth is renewed like the eagle's.

6. **PSALM 107:20** He sent His word and healed them, and delivered them from their destructions.

7. **PROVERBS 3:7,8** Do not be wise in your own eyes; fear the Lord and shun evil. This will bring health to your body and nourishment to your bones. (NIV)

8. **PROVERBS 4:20–22** My son, give attention to my words; incline your ear to my sayings. Do not let them depart from your eyes; keep them in the midst of your heart; for they are life to those who find them, and health to all their flesh.

9. **PROVERBS 16:24** Kind words are like honey—sweet to the soul and healthy for the body. (NLT)

10. **ISAIAH 53:5** But He was wounded for our transgressions, He was bruised for our iniquities; the chastisement for our peace was upon Him, and by His stripes we are healed.

11. **ISAIAH 58:8** Then your light shall break forth like the morning, your healing shall spring forth speedily, and your righteousness shall go before you; the glory of the Lord shall be your rear guard.

12. **JEREMIAH 17:14** Heal me, O Lord, and I shall be healed; save me, and I shall be saved, for You are my praise.

13. **MALACHI 4:2** But for you who fear my name, the Sun of Righteousness will rise with healing in his wings. And you will go free, leaping with joy like calves let out to pasture. (NLT)

14. **MATTHEW 4:23,24** And Jesus went about all Galilee, teaching in their synagogues, preaching the gospel of the kingdom, and healing all kinds of sickness and all kinds of disease among the people. Then His fame went throughout all Syria; and they brought to Him all sick people who were afflicted with various diseases and torments, and those who were demon-possessed, epileptics, and paralytics; and He healed them.

15. **MATTHEW 8:1–3** When He had come down from the mountain, great multitudes followed Him. And behold, a leper came and worshiped Him, saying, "Lord, if You are willing, You can make me clean." Then Jesus put out His hand and touched him, saying, "I am willing; be cleansed." Immediately his leprosy was cleansed.

16. **MATTHEW 8:5–13** Now when Jesus had entered Capernaum, a centurion came to Him, pleading with Him, saying, "Lord, my servant is lying at home paralyzed, dreadfully tormented." And Jesus said to him, "I will come and heal him." The centurion answered and said, "Lord, I am not worthy that You should come under my roof. But only speak a word, and my servant will be healed. For I also am a man under authority, having soldiers under me. And I say to this one, 'Go,' and he goes; and to another, 'Come,' and he comes; and to my

servant, 'Do this,' and he does it." When Jesus heard it, He marveled, and said to those who followed, "Assuredly, I say to you, I have not found such great faith, not even in Israel! And I say to you that many will come from east and west, and sit down with Abraham, Isaac, and Jacob in the kingdom of heaven. But the sons of the kingdom will be cast out into outer darkness. There will be weeping and gnashing of teeth." Then Jesus said to the centurion, "Go your way; and as you have believed, so let it be done for you." And his servant was healed that same hour.

17. **MATTHEW 8:14,15** Now when Jesus had come into Peter's house, He saw his wife's mother lying sick with a fever. So He touched her hand, and the fever left her. And she arose and served them.

18. **MATTHEW 8:16,17** When evening had come, they brought to Him many who were demon-possessed. And He cast out the spirits with a word, and healed all who were sick, that it might be fulfilled which was spoken by Isaiah the prophet, saying: "He Himself took our infirmities and bore our sicknesses."

19. **MATTHEW 9:35** Then Jesus went about all the cities and villages, teaching in their synagogues, preaching the gospel of the kingdom, and healing every sickness and every disease among the people.

20. **MATTHEW 12:15** But when Jesus knew it, He withdrew from there. And great multitudes followed Him, and He healed them all.

21. **MATTHEW 14:14** And when Jesus went out He saw a great multitude; and He was moved with compassion for them, and healed their sick.

22. **MATTHEW 15:28** Then Jesus answered and said to her, "O woman, great is your faith! Let it be to you as you desire." And her daughter was healed from that very hour.

23. **MATTHEW 15:30** Then great multitudes came to Him, having with them the lame, blind, mute, maimed, and many others; and they laid them down at Jesus' feet, and He healed them.

24. **MARK 5:25–34** Now a certain woman had a flow of blood for twelve years, and had suffered many things from many physicians. She had spent all that she had and was no better, but rather grew worse. When she heard about Jesus, she came behind Him in the crowd and touched His garment. For she said, "If only I may touch His clothes, I shall be made well." Immediately the fountain of her blood was dried up, and she felt in her body that she was healed of the affliction. And Jesus, immediately knowing in Himself that power had gone out of Him, turned around in the crowd and said, "Who touched My clothes?" But His disciples said to Him, "You see the multitude thronging You, and You say, "Who touched Me?" And He looked around to see her who had done this thing. But the woman, fearing and trembling, knowing what had happened to her, came and fell down before Him and told Him the whole truth. And He said to her, "Daughter, your faith has made you well. Go in peace, and be healed of your affliction."

25. **MARK 10:46–52** Now they came to Jericho. As He went out of Jericho with His disciples and a great multitude, blind Bartimaeus, the son of Timaeus, sat by the road begging. And when he heard that it was Jesus of Nazareth, he began to cry out and say, "Jesus, Son of David, have mercy on me!" Then many warned him to be quiet; but he cried out all the more, "Son of David, have mercy on me!" So Jesus stood still and commanded him to be called. Then they called the blind man, saying to him, "Be of good cheer. Rise, He is calling you." And throwing aside his garment, he rose and came to Jesus. So Jesus answered and said to him, "What do you want Me to do for you?" The blind man said to Him, "Rabboni, that I may receive my sight." Then Jesus said to him, "Go your way; your faith has made you well." And immediately he received his sight and followed Jesus on the road.

26. **LUKE 4:18** "The Spirit of the Lord is upon Me, because He has anointed Me to preach the gospel to the poor; He has sent Me to heal the brokenhearted, to proclaim liberty to the captives and recovery of sight to the blind, to set at liberty those who are oppressed.

27. **LUKE 4:38–40** Now He arose from the synagogue and entered Simon's house. But Simon's wife's mother was sick with a high fever, and they made request of Him concerning her. So He stood over her and rebuked the fever, and it left her. And immediately she arose and served them. When the sun was setting, all those who had any that were sick with various diseases brought them to Him; and He laid His hands on every one of them and healed them.

28. **LUKE 6:19** And the whole multitude sought to touch Him, for power went out from Him and healed them all.

29. **LUKE 8:41–55** And behold, there came a man named Jairus, and he was a ruler of the synagogue. And he fell down at Jesus' feet and begged Him to come to his house, for he had an only daughter about twelve years of age, and she was dying. But as He went, the multitudes thronged Him. Now a woman, having a flow of blood for twelve years, who had spent all her livelihood on physicians and could not be healed by any, came from behind and touched the border of His garment. And immediately her flow of blood stopped. And Jesus said, "Who touched Me?" When all denied it, Peter and those with him said, "Master, the multitudes throng and press You, and You say, "Who touched Me?"' But Jesus said, "Somebody touched Me, for I perceived power going out from Me." Now when the woman saw that she was not hidden, she came trembling; and falling down before Him, she declared to Him in the presence of all the people the reason she had touched Him and how she was healed immediately. And He said to her, "Daughter, be of good cheer; your faith has made you well. Go in peace." While He was still speaking, someone came from the ruler of the synagogue's house, saying to him, "Your daughter is dead. Do not trouble the Teacher." But when Jesus heard it, He answered him, saying, "Do not be afraid; only believe, and she will be made well." When He came into the house, He permitted no one to go in except Peter, James, and John, and the father and mother of the girl. Now all wept and mourned for her; but He said, "Do not weep; she is not dead, but sleeping." And they ridiculed Him, knowing that she was dead. But He put them all outside, took her by the

hand and called, saying, "Little girl, arise." Then her spirit returned, and she arose immediately. And He commanded that she be given something to eat.

30. **LUKE 9:1,2** Then He called His twelve disciples to-gether and gave them power and authority over all de-mons, and to cure diseases. He sent them to preach the kingdom of God and to heal the sick.

31. **LUKE 9:11** But when the multitudes knew it, they followed Him; and He received them and spoke to them about the kingdom of God, and healed those who had need of healing.

32. **JOHN 5:1–9** After this there was a feast of the Jews, and Jesus went up to Jerusalem. Now there is in Jerusalem by the Sheep Gate a pool, which is called in Hebrew, Bethesda, having five porches. In these lay a great multitude of sick people, blind, lame, paralyzed, waiting for the moving of the water. For an angel went down at a certain time into the pool and stirred up the water; then whoever stepped in first, after the stirring of the water, was made well of whatever disease he had. Now a certain man was there who had an infirmity thirty-eight years. When Jesus saw him lying there, and knew that he already had been in that condition a long time, He said to him, "Do you want to be made well?" The sick man answered Him, "Sir, I have no man to put me into the pool when the water is stirred up; but while I am coming, another steps down before me." Jesus said to him, "Rise, take up your bed and walk." And immediately the man was made well, took up his bed, and walked. And that day was the Sabbath.

33. **ACTS 3:2–8** And a certain man lame from his mother's womb was carried, whom they laid daily at the gate of the temple which is called Beautiful, to ask alms from those who entered the temple; who, seeing Peter and John about to go into the temple, asked for alms. And fixing his eyes on him, with John, Peter said, "Look at us." So he gave them his attention, expecting to receive something from them. Then Peter said, "Silver and gold I do not have, but what I do have I give you: In the name of Jesus Christ of Nazareth, rise up and walk." And he took him by the right hand and lifted him up, and immediately his feet and ankle bones received strength. So he, leaping up, stood and walked and entered the temple with them—walking, leaping, and praising God.

34. **ACTS 5:16** Also a multitude gathered from the surrounding cities to Jerusalem, bringing sick people and those who were tormented by unclean spirits, and they were all healed.

35. **ACTS 14:8–10** And in Lystra a certain man without strength in his feet was sitting, a cripple from his mother's womb, who had never walked. This man heard Paul speaking. Paul, observing him intently and seeing that he had faith to be healed, said with a loud voice, "Stand up straight on your feet!" And he leaped and walked.

36. **ACTS 19:11,12** Now God worked unusual miracles by the hands of Paul, so that even handkerchiefs or aprons were brought from his body to the sick, and the diseases left them and the evil spirits went out of them.

37. **2 CORINTHIANS 4:7–10** But we have this treasure in earthen vessels, that the excellence of the power may be of God and not of us. We are hard-pressed on every side, yet not crushed; we are perplexed, but not in despair; persecuted, but not forsaken; struck down, but not destroyed—always carrying about in the body the dying of the Lord Jesus, that the life of Jesus also may be manifested in our body.

38. **1 THESSALONIANS 5:23** And may the God of peace Himself sanctify you through and through [separate you from profane things, make you pure and wholly consecrated to God]; and may your spirit and soul and body be preserved sound and complete [and found] blameless at the coming of our Lord Jesus Christ (the Messiah). (AMP)

39. **JAMES 5:14–16** Is anyone among you sick? Let him call for the elders of the church, and let them pray over him, anointing him with oil in the name of the Lord. And the prayer of faith will save the sick, and the Lord will raise him up. And if he has committed sins, he will be forgiven. Confess your trespasses to one another, and pray for one another, that you may be healed. The effective, fervent prayer of a righteous man avails much.

40. **1 PETER 2:24** Who Himself bore our sins in His own body on the tree, that we, having died to sins, might live for righteousness—by whose stripes you were healed.

41. **3 JOHN 2** Beloved, I wish above all things that thou mayest prosper and be in health, even as thy soul prospereth. (KJV)

Healing and Wholeness for Spiritual and Emotional Needs

1. **PSALM 103:2,3,5** Bless the Lord, O my soul, and forget not all His benefits: who forgives all your iniquities, who heals all your diseases, who satisfies your mouth with good things, so that your youth is renewed like the eagle's.

2. **PSALM 147:3** He heals the brokenhearted and binds up their wounds.

3. **PROVERBS 12:18** Reckless words pierce like a sword, but the tongue of the wise brings healing. (NIV)

4. **PROVERBS 16:24** Kind words are like honey—sweet to the soul and healthy for the body. (NLT)

5. **PROVERBS 18:21** Death and life are in the power of the tongue, and those who love it will eat its fruit.

6. **ISAIAH 53:5** But He was wounded for our transgressions, He was bruised for our iniquities; the chastisement for our peace was upon Him, and by His stripes we are healed.

7. **ISAIAH 58:8** Then your light shall break forth like the morning, your healing shall spring forth speedily, and your righteousness shall go before you; the glory of the Lord shall be your rear guard.

8. **ISAIAH 61:1** "The Spirit of the Lord God is upon Me, because the Lord has anointed Me to preach good tidings to the poor; He has sent Me to heal the brokenhearted,

to proclaim liberty to the captives, and the opening of the prison to those who are bound.

9. **JEREMIAH 17:14** Heal me, O Lord, and I shall be healed; save me, and I shall be saved, for You are my praise.

10. **LUKE 4:18** "The Spirit of the Lord is upon Me, because He has anointed Me to preach the gospel to the poor; He has sent Me to heal the brokenhearted, to proclaim liberty to the captives and recovery of sight to the blind, to set at liberty those who are oppressed.

11. **JOHN 3:16,17** For God so loved the world that He gave His only begotten Son, that whoever believes in Him should not perish but have everlasting life. For God did not send His Son into the world to condemn the world, but that the world through Him might be saved.

12. **JOHN 4:7–15** A woman of Samaria came to draw water. Jesus said to her, "Give Me a drink." For His disciples had gone away into the city to buy food. Then the woman of Samaria said to Him, "How is it that You, being a Jew, ask a drink from me, a Samaritan woman?" For Jews have no dealings with Samaritans. Jesus answered and said to her, "If you knew the gift of God, and who it is who says to you, 'Give Me a drink,' you would have asked Him, and He would have given you living water." The woman said to Him, "Sir, You have nothing to draw with, and the well is deep. Where then do You get that living water? Are You greater than our father Jacob, who gave us the well, and drank from it himself, as well as his sons and his livestock?" Jesus answered and said to her, "Whoever drinks of this water

will thirst again, but whoever drinks of the water that I shall give him will never thirst. But the water that I shall give him will become in him a fountain of water springing up into everlasting life." The woman said to Him, "Sir, give me this water, that I may not thirst, nor come here to draw."

13. **JOHN 11:25,26** Jesus said to her, "I am the resurrection and the life. He who believes in Me, though he may die, he shall live. And whoever lives and believes in Me shall never die. Do you believe this?"

14. **2 CORINTHIANS 5:17** Therefore, if anyone is in Christ, he is a new creation; old things have passed away; behold, all things have become new.

15. **1 THESSALONIANS 5:23** And may the God of peace Himself sanctify you through and through [separate you from profane things, make you pure and wholly consecrated to God]; and may your spirit and soul and body be preserved sound and complete [and found] blameless at the coming of our Lord Jesus Christ (the Messiah). (AMP)

16. **1 PETER 2:24** Who Himself bore our sins in His own body on the tree, that we, having died to sins, might live for righteousness—by whose stripes you were healed.

Healing and Wholeness for Financial Distress and Lack

1. **GENESIS 8:22** While the earth remains, seedtime and harvest, cold and heat, winter and summer, and day and night shall not cease.

2. **PSALM 103:2,3,5** Bless the Lord, O my soul, and forget not all His benefits: who forgives all your iniquities, who heals all your diseases, who satisfies your mouth with good things, so that your youth is renewed like the eagle's.

3. **PROVERBS 3:9,10** Honor the Lord with your wealth, with the firstfruits of all your crops; then your barns will be filled to overflowing, and your vats will brim over with new wine. (NIV)

4. **ISAIAH 61:1** "The Spirit of the Lord God is upon Me, because the Lord has anointed Me to preach good tidings to the poor; He has sent Me to heal the brokenhearted, to proclaim liberty to the captives, and the opening of the prison to those who are bound.

5. **JEREMIAH 17:14** Heal me, O Lord, and I shall be healed; save me, and I shall be saved, for You are my praise.

6. **MALACHI 3:10,11** Bring all the tithes into the storehouse, that there may be food in My house, and try Me now in this," says the Lord of hosts, "If I will not open for you the windows of heaven and pour out for you such blessing that there will not be room enough to receive it.

   And I will rebuke the devourer for your sakes, so that he will not destroy the fruit of your ground, nor shall the vine fail to bear fruit for you in the field," says the Lord of hosts.

7. **LUKE 4:18** "The Spirit of the Lord is upon Me, because He has anointed Me to preach the gospel to the poor;

He has sent Me to heal the brokenhearted, to proclaim liberty to the captives and recovery of sight to the blind, to set at liberty those who are oppressed.

8. **LUKE 6:38** If you give, you will receive. Your gift will return to you in full measure, pressed down, shaken together to make room for more, and running over. Whatever measure you use in giving—large or small—it will be used to measure what is given back to you. (NLT)

9. **PHILIPPIANS 4:19** And my God shall supply all your need according to His riches in glory by Christ Jesus.

10. **3 JOHN 2** Beloved, I wish above all things that thou mayest prosper and be in health, even as thy soul prospereth. (KJV)

Protection and Deliverance from Evil Attacks

1. **PSALM 23:4** Yea, though I walk through the valley of the shadow of death, I will fear no evil; for You are with me; Your rod and Your staff, they comfort me.

2. **PSALM 57:1** Be merciful to me, O God, be merciful to me! For my soul trusts in You; and in the shadow of Your wings I will make my refuge, until these calamities have passed by.

3. **PSALM 91:1–16** He who dwells in the secret place of the Most High shall abide under the shadow of

the Almighty. I will say of the Lord, "He is my refuge and my fortress; My God, in Him I will trust."

Surely He shall deliver you from the snare of the fowler and from the perilous pestilence. He shall cover you with His feathers, and under His wings you shall take refuge; His truth shall be your shield and buckler. You shall not be afraid of the terror by night, nor of the arrow that flies by day, nor of the pestilence that walks in darkness, nor of the destruction that lays waste at noonday.

A thousand may fall at your side, and ten thousand at your right hand; but it shall not come near you. Only with your eyes shall you look, and see the reward of the wicked.

Because you have made the Lord, who is my refuge, even the Most High, your dwelling place, no evil shall befall you, nor shall any plague come near your dwelling; for He shall give His angels charge over you, to keep you in all your ways. In their hands they shall bear you up, lest you dash your foot against a stone. You shall tread upon the lion and the cobra, the young lion and the serpent you shall trample underfoot.

"Because he has set his love upon Me, therefore I will deliver him; I will set him on high, because he has known My name. He shall call upon Me, and I will answer him; I will be with him in trouble; I will deliver him and honor him. With long life I will satisfy him, and show him My salvation."

4. **PSALM 118:6** The Lord is on my side; I will not fear. What can man do to me?

5.   **PSALM 121:1,2** I will lift up my eyes to the hills—From whence comes my help? My help comes from the Lord, who made heaven and earth.

6.   **JEREMIAH 17:14** Heal me, O Lord, and I shall be healed; save me, and I shall be saved, for You are my praise.

7.   **MARK 16:17,18** And these signs will follow those who believe: In My name they will cast out demons; they will speak with new tongues; they will take up serpents; and if they drink anything deadly, it will by no means hurt them; they will lay hands on the sick, and they will recover.

8.   **LUKE 4:18** "The Spirit of the Lord is upon Me, because He has anointed Me to preach the gospel to the poor; He has sent Me to heal the brokenhearted, to proclaim liberty to the captives and recovery of sight to the blind, to set at liberty those who are oppressed.

9.   **ACTS 5:16** Also a multitude gathered from the surrounding cities to Jerusalem, bringing sick people and those who were tormented by unclean spirits, and they were all healed.

10. **2 CORINTHIANS 4:7–10** But we have this treasure in earthen vessels, that the excellence of the power may be of God and not of us. We are hard-pressed on every side, yet not crushed; we are perplexed, but not in despair; persecuted, but not forsaken; struck down, but not destroyed—always carrying about in the body the dying of the Lord Jesus, that the life of Jesus also may be manifested in our body.

Encouragement and Hope in the Promises of God

1. **PSALM 25:3** Yes, let none who trust and wait hopefully and look for You be put to shame or be disappointed; let them be ashamed who forsake the right or deal treacherously without cause. (AMP)

2. **PSALM 55:22** Cast your burden on the Lord, and He shall sustain you; He shall never permit the righteous to be moved.

3. **PSALM 112:7** He will have no fear of bad news; his heart is steadfast, trusting in the Lord. (NIV)

4. **ISAIAH 43:2** When you pass through the waters, I will be with you; and through the rivers, they shall not overflow you. When you walk through the fire, you shall not be burned, nor shall the flame scorch you.

5. **NAHUM 1:7** The Lord is good, a refuge in times of trouble. He cares for those who trust in him. (NIV)

6. **MATTHEW 17:20** For assuredly, I say to you, if you have faith as a mustard seed, you will say to this mountain, 'Move from here to there,' and it will move; and nothing will be impossible for you."

7. **MARK 11:23–24** For assuredly, I say to you, whoever says to this mountain, "Be removed and be cast into the sea,' and does not doubt in his heart, but believes that those things he says will be done, he will have whatever he says. Therefore I say to you, whatever things you ask

when you pray, believe that you receive them, and you will have them.

8. **LUKE 9:56** For the Son of Man did not come to destroy men's lives but to save them.

9. **LUKE 11:9** So I say to you, ask, and it will be given to you; seek, and you will find; knock, and it will be opened to you.

10. **LUKE 18:1** One day Jesus told his disciples a story to illustrate their need for constant prayer and to show them that they must never give up. (NLT)

11. **JOHN 10:10** The thief does not come except to steal, and to kill, and to destroy. I have come that they may have life, and that they may have it more abundantly.

12. **2 CORINTHIANS 5:17** Therefore, if anyone is in Christ, he is a new creation; old things have passed away; behold, all things have become new.

13. **EPHESIANS 3:20,21** Now to Him who is able to do exceedingly abundantly above all that we ask or think, according to the power that works in us, to Him be glory in the church by Christ Jesus to all generations, forever and ever. Amen.

14. **HEBREWS 4:16** Let us therefore come boldly to the throne of grace, that we may obtain mercy and find grace to help in time of need.

15. **HEBREW 11:1-6** Now faith is the substance of things hoped for, the evidence of things not seen. For

by it the elders obtained a good testimony. By faith we understand that the worlds were framed by the word of God, so that the things which are seen were not made of things which are visible. By faith Abel offered to God a more excellent sacrifice than Cain, through which he obtained witness that he was righteous, God testifying of his gifts; and through it he being dead still speaks. By faith Enoch was taken away so that he did not see death, "and was not found, because God had taken him"; for before he was taken he had this testimony, that he pleased God. But without faith it is impossible to please Him, for he who comes to God must believe that He is, and that He is a rewarder of those who diligently seek Him.

16. **HEBREWS 13:8** Jesus Christ is the same yesterday, today, and forever.

17. **JAMES 1:17** Every good gift and every perfect gift is from above, and comes down from the Father of lights, with whom there is no variation or shadow of turning.

18. **1 JOHN 3:8** For this purpose the Son of God was manifested, that He might destroy the works of the devil.

19. **1 JOHN 4:4** You are of God, little children, and have overcome them, because He who is in you is greater than he who is in the world.

20. **1 JOHN 5:14** Now this is the confidence that we have in Him, that if we ask anything according to His will, He hears us.

Healing and Wholeness for the Nations and the Body of Christ

1. **2 CHRONICLES 7:14** If My people who are called by My name will humble themselves, and pray and seek My face, and turn from their wicked ways, then I will hear from heaven, and will forgive their sin and heal their land.

2. **ISAIAH 57:18,19** I have seen what they do, but I will heal them anyway! I will lead them and comfort those who mourn. Then words of praise will be on their lips. May they have peace, both near and far, for I will heal them all," says the Lord.

3. **JEREMIAH 30:17** For I will restore health to you and heal you of your wounds,' says the Lord, "because they called you an outcast saying: "This is Zion; no one seeks her."

4. **JEREMIAH 33:6** Behold, I will bring it health and healing; I will heal them and reveal to them the abundance of peace and truth.

PRAYER OF CONFESSION

Here is a sample prayer that you can use to confess some of the many healing promises from God's Word, and to help you picture yourself as He sees you...healed and whole. I encourage you to find other Scriptures that are meaningful to you and encourage yourself in the Lord with them every day. **–RR**

Lord,

Your Word says in Luke 1:37 that **with You** nothing is ever impossible, and that no word *from You* shall be without power or **impossible** of fulfillment. Nothing is too big or too small for Your concern. You're never too busy or too far away from me to intervene when I call on You.

When the woman who had hemorrhaged for 12 years without finding any medical help followed You and touched Your robe, You healed her (Luke 8).

When the Roman centurion came to You and told You his servant was ill, You healed him (Matthew 8).

When Jairus came to You and told You his little girl was dying, You went to their home and healed her (Matthew 9).

When Your friend Lazarus died, You went to his home, comforted his sisters, and cried for the loss of Your friend. Then You healed him, by raising him from the dead (John 11).

When the man brought his demon-possessed son to You, You had compassion on him and healed him, so that he was back in his own mind again. And You healed the broken relationship between the man and his son (Mark 9).

When a man's four friends brought their friend to You because he couldn't walk and was too sick to come to You on his own, You didn't get upset because they lowered him through the roof and interrupted Your preaching. You saw their faith and You healed him (Mark 2).

When a leper came to You—someone who was cast aside by everyone else—and said, "Jesus, I believe You can heal me…if You want to," You said, "Yes, I want to," and You healed him. You forever settled the questions: (1) Do You care that I'm sick? and (2) Do You want me to be well? (Matthew 8).

When You passed by a blind man begging by the side of the road and You heard him call Your name, "Jesus, son of David, have mercy on me," others tried to shut him up. But not You. You stopped and asked Bartimaeus, "What do you want me to do for you?" He cried, "Lord, I want to see!" and You gave Him sight—spiritual, as well as physical (Mark 10).

You want me to be well…and to live with You forever in Heaven. You know me better than I know myself, and You love me more than I could ever comprehend, so much so that You say in Isaiah 49:15–16 that even if a mother can forget her nursing infant, You will never forget me…that You've inscribed a picture of me on the palms of Your hands. You created me and knew me before time began (Psalm 139) and Your love for me will never end (Jeremiah 31:3). I didn't do anything to make You love me and there's nothing I can ever do to make You *not* love me. Romans 8:38 says that *nothing* can ever separate me from Your unconditional love.

Now You are saying to me, "What do you want me to do for *you*?"

Lord, I want to be healed...of anything and everything that is attacking my body and my life that is not from You. I believe You will do the same for me that You've done for people in the Bible, and that You will do for anyone else through the centuries who will ask You.

When You were on this earth, You went about doing good and healing all those who came to You for help. You never turned away anyone who came to You for healing.

Thank You for healing me now.

RICHARD ROBERTS
ORAL ROBERTS MINISTRIES

Richard Roberts
P.O. Box 2187
Tulsa, OK 74102-2187

www.oralroberts.com

For prayer anytime, call *The Abundant Life Prayer Group* at 918-495-7777, or contact us on the web at **www.oralroberts.com/prayer**.